Coarse Fishing Illustrated

Trevor Housby and Keith Linsell

BARRIE & JENKINS
COMMUNICA · EUROPA

© 1966 by Trevor Housby and Keith Linsell
First published 1966 by Herbert Jenkins Ltd.
2 Clement's Inn, London WC2A 2EP

Reprinted 1969

Reprinted 1972 by Barrie and Jenkins Ltd.
24 Highbury Crescent, London N5 1RX
Reprinted 1975, 1978

ISBN 0 257 66518 8

Printed in Great Britain by
Redwood Burn Limited Trowbridge & Esher

INTRODUCTION

WRITING an easily understandable book on angling is not a particularly simple project, for angling is a complex subject which defies over-simplification. By using many illustrations, however, it is possible to overcome this problem to some extent—as will be clearly seen in the following pages. Readers will notice that I have devoted quite a lot of space to the fish themselves, for I feel that it is extremely important to be able to identify each fish as and when you catch it. This adds considerably to the interest of angling and also helps you to understand the ways of the fish, which is a major step in the right direction—for after a while it will become second nature to identify certain fish with certain waters and swims. This knowledge is invaluable. It constitutes part of the secret of "water lore", which every good fisherman must possess.

The only way to add to this knowledge is to fish hard and long at every opportunity and to think fully about each successive day's sport, so that your past experiences will eventually guide you instinctively to the fish you seek. To develop this instinct fully takes time, and basically it is really a matter of serving an apprenticeship to your sport. If you learn your lessons well, then you will become a master of your craft. If you don't, you will still catch fish—but not of the same size or quality as the angler who has carefully studied the subject.

Most of the methods described and illustrated here are those that have been well tried and tested and are known to be successful. All of them I use myself, and many of my biggest fish have been caught on tackle described in the text. One of the best principles to adopt when fishing is to keep the tackle as simple and gadget-free as possible. Carp fishermen, for instance, often dispense entirely with floats and weights and tie the hook directly to the line. This is undoubtedly the simplest form of terminal tackle and yet it is highly effective, for at least seventy-five per cent of the biggest carp ever caught in this country have been taken on it—among them being the present British Record carp of 44 lb.

Not only is it possible to learn by your own experience but you can also learn by watching others. This was something I realized very early in life, and by watching points I gained a great deal of theoretical knowledge which was easily adapted to suit conditions as I found them.

When it comes to choosing a new rod or reel, always purchase the best that you can afford. Don't make the common mistake of buying cheap or flashy equipment. Instead, decide beforehand what sort of fish you are mainly interested in and choose your tackle accordingly. Also make sure that you buy equipment for which spare parts and replacements will be easily obtainable. In this respect, your local tackle-dealer can help you considerably.

Finally, I would like to say that in writing this book I have tried to impart as much knowledge as possible to the reader. Keith Linsell's excellent illustrations have helped me considerably in this project and I am confident that, by following the instructions and the diagrams, it should be possible for any reader to float fish, leger or spin without problems, able to hold his own on any water and with any species of fish.

T. R. HOUSBY

Barbel (*Barbus barbus*)

In many ways the barbel resembles a long lean common carp, which is understandable for both fish belong to the same family. Unlike the true carp, however, which prefers still or slow moving waters, the barbel is a fish of the faster rivers and lives happily in the heaviest of currents.

In shape the barbel is a round-bodied fish with large powerful fins and a wide strong tail, obviously well adapted for a life which is spent in fast water. Its eyes are rather small and are set high up on its head.

Barbel take their name from the barbels or feelers that sprout from their upper and lower lips. These barbels help the fish to root round for food in the gravel and mud on the river bottom.

Barbel grow to quite a large size and although a ten-pounder can be looked upon as a good specimen, it is by no means an exceptional fish and the rod-caught record stands at 14 lb. 6 oz. Fish up to and possibly over 20 lb. are known to exist and several over the record size have been foul-hooked during the close season by salmon anglers.

Once hooked, the barbel puts up a magnificent fight and on the Hampshire Avon, where there are many big barbel, I have watched anglers play barbel for anything up to half an hour before the fish have been ready for the net.

Unfortunately, barbel have a rather limited and local distribution. In the south of England, the main barbel waters are the Thames, the Kennet, the Lea, the Avon and the Dorset Stour. In the north Yorkshire rivers like the Ouse, Nidd and Swale are the most likely places to catch a barbel. There has, however, been a minor restocking programme carried out on one or two waters and with luck barbel will become more widespread in years to come.

To be able to live, the barbel must have clean, unpolluted water and, unfortunately, many rivers which would otherwise be suitable barbel waters have a high rate of pollution.

Barbel can be caught both by float fishing and legering and to get the best results it pays to use both methods, depending, of course, on prevailing water conditions. In heavy flood water or in weir pools leger is usually best, but in fast streamy swims between weed beds a float can be used to carry the bait down to the waiting fish.

Almost any bait will catch a barbel but the favourites are worm, maggot, cheese paste and bread flake.

Bleak (*Alburnus alburnus*)

The bleak is a silvery little fish which is very common in many of our rivers. The Thames and its tributaries are infested with hordes of these active, fast moving, little fish which make a complete nuisance of themselves by gorging baits intended for larger and more sporting species.

Bleak never grow very large and the largest specimens do not reach 8 in. In general colour and shape they are somewhat similar to dace, except that the body of the bleak is rather flat, while that of the true dace is round.

When there is nothing else about, bleak fishing can be great fun, and providing your reactions are fast enough you will be able to catch dozens of bleak at a sitting. Maggots are the best bait for bleak but they will also take worm or bread. To get the best sport very light float tackle should be used.

Bleak make first-class livebait for pike or perch fishing and some of the biggest perch fall to a nice lively bleak fished on leger tackle.

Common or Bronze Bream (*Abramis brama*)

The common bream is the largest of our two breams and is a close relative to the carp, as can be seen by the hump-backed, deep-bodied appearance of the adult fish.

In colour common bream have bronze or olive green sides. The fins are large and rather bluish in colour and the underparts are white. The majority of bream are covered in a layer of thick protective slime which drips off and covers everything that it touches. Keep-nets and landing nets which have been used for holding bream are usually covered in this rather unpleasant substance and unless they are thoroughly washed and dried after use, they will stink the place out for days afterwards.

Generally, the bream is a fish of still waters or slow-flowing waterways, and in places like the Norfolk Broads they are very common and huge catches of a hundredweight or more are common. Bream are also shoal fish and providing you are able to locate and hold the interest of a bream shoal you should be able to catch any amount of good fish, one after the other.

The only real way to keep the shoal in one area is by groundbaiting extensively, preferably with a mixture of bread and bran. Bream experts think nothing of using fifty or more pounds of groundbait at a sitting.

Locating a bream shoal is fairly easy providing you know what to look for. If you see bream rolling on the surface of the water for instance, you can usually catch fish by casting close to the rolling fish. Patches of muddy or disturbed water in an otherwise clear area are another good sign and

BARBEL

BLEAK

COMMON BREAM

providing you drop your bait right into the middle of the disturbed patch, you can expect quite a lot of good sport before the shoals move away.

Worms are probably the best bait for bream fishing but bread paste and maggots can also be deadly. It pays to carry a selection of baits in case the bream happen to be in a fussy mood. Very occasionally, bream will pick up and spit out the bait very quickly. This usually happens when you are using worms and if you add two or three maggots to the point and barb of the hook, the bream can usually be induced to take the bait properly.

When the bream shoals are really on the move, it does not matter whether you use float or leger tackle but when the fish are feeding rather spasmodically it pays to use a light leger and strike at the first indication of a bite.

Bream grow to quite a large size and the record weight stands at 13 lb. 8 oz. This was an exceptional fish, however, and as a rule any bream over 5 lb. can be looked upon as a good catch.

Silver Bream (*Blicca bjoernka*)

Silver bream seldom attain a good weight and the average specimen weighs between 12 oz. and 16 oz. Larger fish do exist, however, and the rod-caught record silver bream weighed over 4 lb. This fish was naturally an exceptional specimen and generally any silver bream of 2 lb. or more in weight can be looked upon as a big fish.

Silver bream are rather local in habitat and apart from one or two ponds and lakes which have been specially stocked, they are confined almost exclusively to a few slow-moving rivers in eastern England.

No special tackle or baits are needed to catch these fish and the majority of specimens recorded have been caught by anglers fishing for roach or bronze bream.

Carp (*Cyprinus carpio*)

Although there are several varieties of carp in British waters, they are all the same species.

Probably the most beautiful variety is the common or wild carp which has a widespread distribution over the country. As the illustration on the opposite page shows, the common carp is a fully scaled fish, each scale neatly overlapping its neighbour. In colour the common carp is usually dark olive on the back with rich golden bronze sides and orange yellow underparts.

The mirror carp is a much more bulky looking fish than the long lean wild carp and as far as fighting ability is concerned, the common carp can

usually be relied upon to put up a dazzling display, whereas the chubby thickset mirror carp tends to rely more upon sheer bulk than speed. The name mirror carp is derived from the large mirror-like scales which run down the lateral line in the centre of the fish's side. These and a few scattered scales are the only scales that the mirror carp possess and the remainder of the fish is covered in thick tough skin.

Mirror carp vary considerably in colour from one water to another but are generally dark orange or chestnut on the side with light coloured underparts. The back of this fish is normally dark slatey blue.

Another variety is the leather carp, which is completely scaleless. Golden carp and other escapees from aquariums or ornamental waters are also found "free" in small numbers.

Carp can grow to an enormous size and the record fish, which weighed 44 lb., was taken by that well-known angler and author, Mr. Richard Walker. A number of other carp over 30 lb. have also been recorded and nowadays a 20-pounder is looked upon as a good but not exceptional catch. Not all carp waters produce heavy fish and in some a 6 lb. carp is a good one.

In recent years carp fishing has become popular. In consequence, many new techniques have been devised. Some of these ideas are extremely technical and my advice to any would-be carp angler is to stick to normal weightless leger tackle. Owing to the large size of an average carp it is essential to use a fairly powerful rod with a line to match.

Carp can be caught on a variety of baits but bread paste is as good as any. Worm and potato baits can also be used to good effect. Many fine carp have been caught on maggots.

Chub (*Leuciscus cephalus*)

The chub is a handsome elongated fish which is very common in many rivers and is found in some canals and lakes. When seen in the water the chub gives the impression of being a bulky fish, mainly because its head is large and its wide, heavy scales tend to make it look larger than it actually is.

In colour the adult chub is silver with a distinct brassy tint to its scales. Its back is greenish black and the dorsal and tail fins are bluish grey, while its pectoral, pelvic and anal fins are crimson.

Chub have many local nicknames, the commonest of which are chevin, chavender and loggerhead.

Chub grow to quite a respectable size and each season a few fish between 6 and 7 lb. are caught. The record fish weighed over 10 lb. On average, however, the majority of chub that are caught

SILVER BREAM

MIRROR & COMMON CARP

CHUB

weigh 2 or 3 lb. and a 5-pounder can be classed as a really good catch.

There are very few baits that will not catch chub and large specimens have even been caught on live-bait and spoons, baits intended for pike. For general use, however, bread, cheese or worms make the best chub baits—but garden slugs, cray-fish and a score of other baits can be used to good effect.

Even a small chub is capable of putting up quite a decent battle when hooked and if you intend to fish in waters which are known to hold chub of specimen size, you should use fairly strong tackle—for big chub have a habit of making a determined dash for the nearest obstruction. Unless your tackle is capable of manhandling them away from the snags, you will lose far more fish than you land.

Crucian Carp (*Carassius carassius*)

Crucian carp are often mistaken for small com-mon carp but the absence of barbels on the mouth of the crucian immediately distinguishes it from the true carp and its varieties.

Originally, crucian carp were introduced into this country from eastern Europe and unlike the common carp, which is widely distributed, the crucian has rather a local distribution and is usually only found in estate ponds and lakes which have been specially stocked. There are a few crucian carp in the Thames.

Like most carp the crucian is a shy fish and bites very cautiously. Consequently it takes a good ang-ler to catch them consistently. The record crucian carp weighed between 4 and 5 lb. and a 3-pounder is an exceptionally good specimen.

Owing to their small average size light tackle can be used to catch these fish and the majority of anglers who specialize in catching crucian carp use roach tackle. Crucians can be caught either with leger or float tackle.

Bread, worms and maggots are the best crucian carp baits—with a bias towards maggots.

Dace (*Leuciscus leuciscus*)

The dace is an extremely active river fish which is usually found in the faster swims, particularly during the summer and autumn months. In the winter they have a tendency to drop back into deeper swims but even then they usually choose a place with a fair current running through it.

In colour dace are basically silver on the sides with darkish green or brown backs. The fins are tinted with yellow or pale pink.

Dace never grow much larger than 1 lb. in weight. Although the record stands at 1½ lb., if you catch a specimen weighing 12 to 14 oz. then you have a fish to be proud of.

Dace bite very sharply and unless your reactions are extremely fast you will miss most of the bites that come your way. By using a tip action roach or match rod which is made for fast striking you will catch more fish than you would with a floppy or slow actioned rod.

Dace fishing can be great fun but to get the best out of it you should float fish with a very light bird or porcupine quill float.

The best baits for dace fishing are worms, mag-gots and hempseed. Hemp is particularly good and on the lower reaches of the Thames where there are vast numbers of sizeable dace, many of the regular anglers use hempseed exclusively.

Dace are mainly surface or midwater feeders, although occasionally the largest fish will sink down and feed on or close to the bottom.

Eels (*Anguilla anguilla*)

Sooner or later most anglers catch an eel, usually quite a small one which wriggles and squirms and winds the line up into a nasty slimy ball. Because of this the majority of anglers take an instant dislike to all eels and never bother to fish for them seriously. This is a pity for there are some very big eels to be found in various waters through-out this country and these can provide some first-class sport. There is no mistaking an eel even if you have never seen one before, for its snake-like appearance and thick body slime identify it im-mediately.

Eels are extremely strong and will fight to the bitter end. Even on really heavy tackle an eel of three or more pounds will put up a fantastic battle, nor does the battle end when the creature is ashore for eels are reasonably well at home out of the water and, being extremely slippery, they are difficult to handle. Most regular eel anglers take along a sack. They drop their eels in the sack, cut the line, tie on a new hook and resume operations, retrieving the hooks when the eels are dealt with at home.

Small eels will feed throughout the day but as a rule the larger specimens are night feeders and seldom venture far from their holes until the sun begins to set. During the night they will wander for considerable distances in search of food and by fishing after dark with suitable baits, you will stand a very good chance of catching some fine eels.

Large worms are probably the best all round bait to use, but unfortunately these can be swal-lowed by small eels and for every decent sized specimen you catch on worm, you will probably

CRUCIAN CARP

DACE

EEL

land a dozen "bootlace" eels. To avoid these pests it is best to use a small dead fish as bait. Almost any fish will do but shiny fish such as roach or rudd seem definitely to attract the bigger eels.

The ideal length of a deadbait for eels is something between 4 in. and 6 in. Leger is the best method. Remember that an eel is a cautious feeder so give it plenty of time to get the bait inside its mouth. If you strike too soon at a biting fish you will probably snatch the bait out of its jaws and frighten it so badly that it will not feed again for the rest of the night.

Gudgeon (*Gobio gobio*)

Despite the fact that even a big gudgeon weighs little more than 2 or 3 oz., these fish are very popular with anglers of all ages. For one thing they bite in a vigorous, determined manner and for another they will fight with all the strength their tiny bodies can muster.

In appearance the gudgeon is very similar to a barbel and very small barbel are often confused with big gudgeon and vice versa. Gudgeon have only two barbels or whiskers whereas barbel have four, and the sides of a gudgeon are much more silvery and have large dark blotches. These are absent on the sides of a barbel.

At one time gudgeon fishing parties were very popular but nowadays most of the gudgeon that are caught are hooked by anglers who are bottom fishing with maggot, paste or worm baited hooks. Gudgeon make first-class livebait for pike and perch fishing and in many areas they are in great demand as bait for these two predatory fish.

Gudgeon are basically shoal fish and where you catch one you will usually catch more. The nicest way of catching these fish is with ultra-light float tackle, but leger can be used as well. Gudgeon can often be attracted to a swim if the bottom of the river or pond is thoroughly disturbed.

Perch (*Perca fluviatilis*)

The perch is undoubtedly one of the most handsome fish in British waters and it is a favourite with a great many anglers, particularly those of the younger generation. Small perch are so easy to catch that they can become a real nuisance but the larger fish are a completely different proposition. It takes a clever and careful angler to catch one of these cunning and cautious creatures.

Perch are common in nearly all parts of the British Isles and although many waters contain only small stunted fish, others in the same area will produce perch of specimen size. There is no mistaking a perch when you catch one for its humped back, spiky dorsal fin and heavily striped sides quickly give it away.

Studies of the habits of big perch indicate that they prefer the deepest water particularly during periods of cold weather. There are exceptions to the rule but generally it pays to fish in the deepest water you can find. Perch also like to live close to snags and if you can find a deep hole close to a fallen tree or near some lock gates, then you may well have a good day's perch fishing.

Small perch can be caught on almost any sort of tackle but for the larger fish a running leger baited either with a large worm or small live fish is best. Perch will also chase and attack various artificial lures and a day's spinning with light tackle can be a most pleasant and rewarding way of fishing.

Perch grow to approximately 5 lb. in weight but the average run of fish can be measured in ounces. Fish of between 1 and 2 lb. are good. Any fish of 3 lb. or over can be looked upon as a fish of a lifetime, for few anglers manage to catch perch much above this weight

The sharp spines of the first dorsal fin can scratch or cut an unwary hand, but they contain no poison of any description.

Pike (*Esox lucius*)

It is only necessary to look at a pike to see that it is a natural hunter, for its long lean shape, large head and huge teeth-filled jaws immediately show it to be a predator.

In colour pike vary considerably from one water to another. Specimens from cloudy gravel pits are often sandy looking monsters, whilst pike from clear water lakes or rivers are usually very green with bright primrose-coloured blotches dappling their sides.

Pike grow to a great size, particularly in remote waters, and specimens up to 53 lb. have been caught in Ireland, a country which is famous for its big pike. In England, the largest recorded specimen weighed 37 lb. 8 oz., but it is certain that much larger pike live in our waters.

Good quality pike fishing is fairly easy to come by for many gravel pits are well stocked with big pike and often these man-made lakes can be fished for 2 or 3 shillings a day. Many rivers and canals also hold pike, although as a rule they do not grow as large as the stillwater specimens.

Pike are rather lazy fish and although they are quite capable of catching their food by speed alone, they much prefer to ambush their prey. For this reason it pays to fish for them in the vicinity of reed beds or other obstructions which provide shelter for the lurking fish.

GUDGEON

PERCH

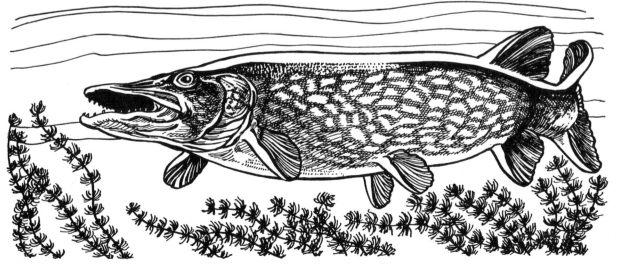

PIKE

Although pike do not fight as hard as carp, it is often necessary to use heavy tackle, particularly if you intend to use live or deadbaits, for the continual strain of casting out these heavy baits will soon ruin a light outfit. If you intend to spin for your fish with light artificial baits you can safely employ lighter tackle, but do not make the common mistake of using a rod and line which is too light, for if you do manage to hook a bigger than average specimen the chances are it will break either the rod or the line.

As a general rule it can be said that the biggest pike will be found in the deepest water in normal lakes, ponds and rivers. It is advisable, therefore, for the pike fisherman to search for and locate the deeper holes in his local pike fishery and to fish them in preference to the shallower swims. There are occasions, of course, when big pike are caught in very shallow water but in my experience this is the exception rather than the rule and usually you will catch plenty of good-sized fish if you stick to the deeper water.

Roach (*Rutilus rutilus*)

A great many anglers fish for roach and nothing else, for these handsome fish with their bright red fins and broad silver sides are extremely attractive fish to catch.

Roach are very common throughout England and in parts of Wales and Scotland. Many a novice angler has begun his angling apprenticeship by catching a netful of small specimens. The larger fish are a different proposition for they are cunning, careful feeders and it takes a good angler to catch roach of over a pound in weight consistently. Even by today's standards, a roach weighing over 2 lb. can be regarded as an exceptional catch and many expert anglers who have made a study of roach fishing techniques never manage to catch a 2-pounder.

Roach have a reputation for being fast biting fish and on hard fished waters or where there are multitudes of stunted undersized fish this is quite true, but the larger specimens usually take the bait in a firm and deliberate manner. Roach of over 2 lb. weight have been caught by carp anglers using large baits and comparatively heavy tackle and on such occasions the fish took the bait with all the dash and speed of a hungry carp.

A 12 ft. match rod or light split cane bottom rod, with a centre pin or fixed spool reel and 3 lb. b.s. line is suggested for float fishing. For leger work something like a 10 ft. two-piece Avon type rod is suitable, with a fixed spool reel and 4½ lb. line. Real roach experts often use a line with a breaking strain of 1½ or 2 lb. but it takes a very clever angler to control big fish on a line as fine as this and personally, I feel it is better to use a heavier line and make sure of landing your fish.

Roach can be caught on a wide variety of baits, but worms, maggots, bread paste, and stewed wheat are perhaps best—and they are easy to procure.

Rudd (*Scardinius erythropthalmus*)

For many years angling writers have referred to the rudd as the "Golden fish of the lakes", a name which I think suits this beautiful fish to perfection, for the adult fish have sides of burnished gold and fins of scarlet which make them one of the most beautiful of all British fish.

Rudd reach a larger average size than roach and although a 2-pounder is a good fish, it is by no means an exceptional specimen, for rudd of 3 lb. or over are caught during the course of most average seasons. Although it is possible to find large rudd in rivers, they are more common in still waters or slow-flowing waterways and the majority of successful rudd fishermen fish either in lakes or dykes.

In Ireland, where there are vast numbers of rudd, several fast rivers hold huge shoals of big rudd, but even there the better quality fish are usually found in the many lakes or loughs.

Rudd have a tendency to feed in the vicintiy of beds of surface weed and if you can manage to locate such a weed patch on your own local rudd waters, it will pay you to fish close to it.

Rudd are shy creatures and it pays to fish carefully and quietly. It is very easy to frighten the school.

No special tackle is required to catch rudd and standard roach equipment is as good as any. If you find that you are losing fish because they are managing to get into the weed and break you up you will naturally step up the strength of your tackle.

Rudd can be caught on most roach baits and the larger fish may also be tempted by a tiny artificial spinner. They feed high in the water except in cold weather and your bait should be 3 ft. or less from your float to start with. If this doesn't bring bites you can increase the depth.

Tench (*Tinca tinca*)

The tench is almost entirely a summer fish and although the occasional specimen can be hooked on a mild winter's day, the best time to try for these fish is during June, July and August.

The tench is a solid, powerful-looking fish with

ROACH

RUDD

TENCH

large, strong, well-shaped fins and a neat small head. In colour they vary considerably from one water to another. Specimens from dark woodland pools can be almost black in colour, while others from more open waters may be greenish bronze with dark golden green sides.

Given the right conditions, tench can grow to quite a large size and the present rod caught record tench weighed a fraction over 9 lb. A 5-pounder is generally regarded as a big fish and anything over 6 lb. can be looked upon as exceptional. The general run of tench is in the region of $1\frac{1}{2}$ to $3\frac{1}{2}$ lb.

Tench are capable of putting up a strong and persistent fight once they are hooked and as they normally feed close to thick weed beds, it is usually necessary to fish with fairly strong tackle otherwise you will lose far more fish than you land. An Avon type rod, 5 or 6 lb. b.s. line and centre pin reel make a good combination for general tench fishing but if extra long casts are required to reach the feeding fish, then it pays to substitute a fixed-spool reel for the centre pin.

Float fishing is perhaps the pleasantest way of fishing for tench, for these fish make the float bob and curtsy for some time before it finally slides away out of sight. Legering, however, often produces bigger fish and for this reason many keen tench fishers invariably use leger tackle.

Tench can be caught on a wide variety of baits, but worms and bread are the most useful. Maggots *will* catch tench, but if there are roach, rudd or perch in the water you will hook these and disturb the swim.

Tench can often be encouraged to feed by the liberal use of groundbait, particularly if you are able to visit the water and groundbait the swim for a week or so before you fish. The best time to catch tench is during the late evening or very early morning and most dedicated tench anglers arrive at the waterside just before dawn.

General Remarks

Most species of British coarse fish can be easily identified, but two pairs need consideration. These are chub/dace and roach/rudd. Colour is always a doubtful guide and should be disregarded.

As far as chub and dace are concerned, the principal difference between the two species is in the shape of the dorsal and anal fins. In the chub these are convex whilst those of the dace are concave. The scales on a chub are also coarser than those of the dace and the chub's head is larger than that of the true dace.

With roach and rudd the most practical and also the quickest way to identify roach from rudd is by looking closely at the lower lip of your catch. If this lip protrudes, then you have caught a rudd and if it recedes then the fish is without doubt a roach. To make absolutely certain, however, you can check on the dorsal fin of the suspect fish. If this fin is set so that it starts just behind the roots of the ventral fins, then the fish is a roach. If the dorsal fin is situated well behind the root of the ventral fins then the fish is a rudd.

It is advisable to check if the fish weighs over 2 lb., for a 2 lb. roach is an exceptional specimen, while a 2 lb. rudd is a good but not exciting catch.

Basically, all coarse fish have the same number of fins. These are the pelvic, pectoral, anal, caudal (tail) and dorsal fins. Certain fish like perch and ruffe have two dorsal fins but most fresh-water fish have only a single dorsal fin. The shape of these fins varies considerably from one species to another, depending mainly upon the type of water the species normally live in. Some fish, carp and barbel in particular, have wide, powerful tails while other fish, perch for instance, have only very small tails. A fish propels itself by movements of its body and tail. The fins (particularly the tail fin) act as rudders and stabilizers.

The body of a fish is covered with an armour plating of scales. These are usually covered with a skin of slime. This gives protection against parasites and bacterial infection, and it is therefore desirable to handle any fish you catch with care, for if you damage this covering and then return the fish to the water, the chances are it will contract some fungoid disease and die.

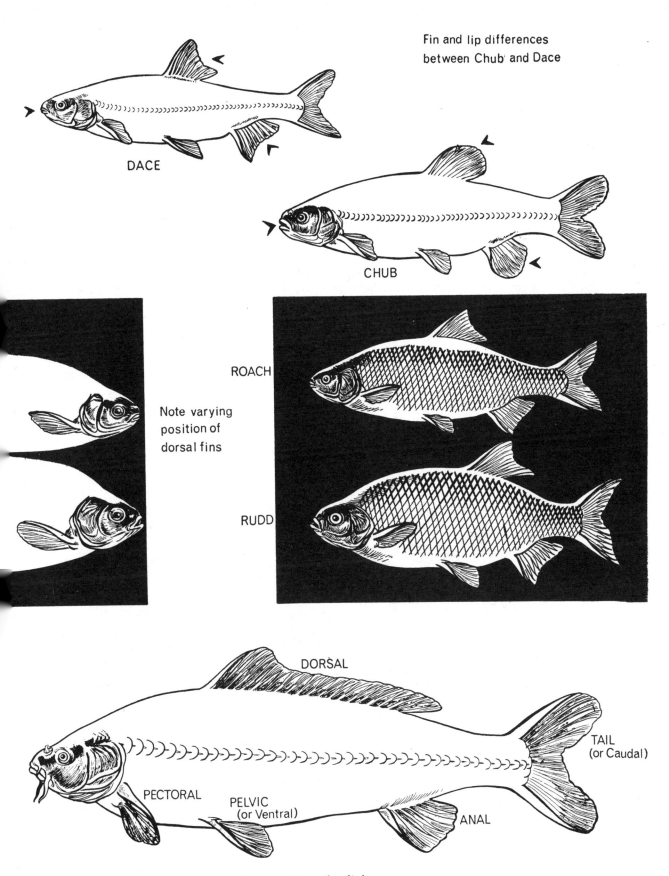

Fin and lip differences between Chub and Dace

DACE

CHUB

Note varying position of dorsal fins

ROACH

RUDD

Basic outline of a fish

DORSAL

TAIL (or Caudal)

PECTORAL

PELVIC (or Ventral)

ANAL

Netting a big fish

Undersized fish are easy enough to land for being small and light in weight they can be lifted straight out of the water and swung ashore. Large fish are a different proposition and the only practical method of landing them is with a landing net. Until you get used to using one of these nets it can be a nerve racking experience to try to enmesh a wildly struggling fish, but with practice the process becomes automatic.

The netting technique is simple but it must be properly learned.

First sink the mesh and the frame of the net and wait patiently till either you or whoever happens to be playing the fish can guide it directly over the sunken net. Once the fish is in this position lift the net quickly but steadily upwards so that the weight of the fish drops into the back or mesh of the net.

At no time must you try to *scoop* the fish out of the water for if you do you frighten it and may well break the line in the process.

If the fish is of medium size you can support its weight on the handle of the net. If it is big it will pay to slide the handle of the net back under your arm and get a firm grip on the frame or mesh of the net with your free hand. This will give a safe hold and avoid breaking the frame or handle of the net.

Once you have the fish safely ashore it must be unhooked as quickly as possible and either returned to the water or placed in a keep-net until you can weigh or photograph it. If the fish is firmly or deeply hooked you will have to use a disgorger or (better still) a pair of forceps to remove the hook.

Forceps can be obtained from most chemists and many of the larger tackle shops.

When the time comes to return the fish to the water you should always handle it with care. Never throw it back for this may well kill or cripple it. Instead, hold it firmly in both hands and slide it gently back into the water. Some fish have difficulty in regaining their balance when they are first returned. If this happens they have to be held upright until they can get up enough strength to swim off.

TENCH

Netting a big fish

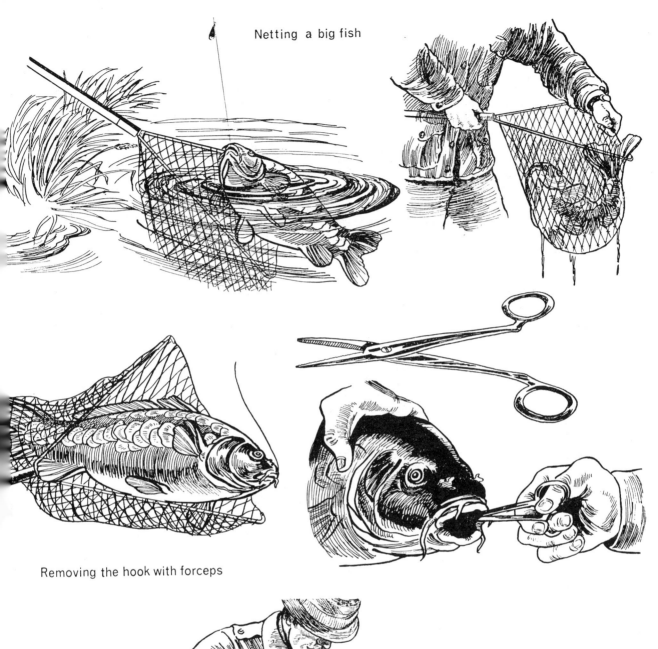

Removing the hook with forceps

Hold the fish
gently but firmly
while returning
it to the water

Tackle

Float rods

Before choosing a new float fishing rod you must first decide which sort of fishing you intend to do, and in what sort of water. For general use in still or slowly moving waters the most popular rod is the "Match Rod", which is ideal for light tackle work and is designed to deal with fast-biting fish such as dace or roach. With this type of rod, the action is in the last 18 in. of the top joint, the rest of the rod being extremely stiff. This tip action is ideal for fast striking, particularly for the smaller species of fish. Match rods vary considerably in length and one of about 12 ft. is suitable for most anglers. Many expert anglers use rods 14 ft. to 16 ft. in length. Match rods are normally made from Spanish reed, light weight steel or hollow fibre-glass. The modern glass and steel rods are lighter than the rather old-fashioned reed rods, but they lack the sweetness of action. They are also much more expensive into the bargain.

For float fishing on faster rivers a special kind of rod must be used. These are known as "Trotting Rods" and are usually 11 ft. long and made up in three sections. The first joint is made of whole cane, while the middle and top sections are of built or split cane. This rod has an action which is ideal for striking a fish that has taken the bait 30 or more yards away. Unfortunately these Avon type rods are rather expensive, but they will amply repay their cost with the amount of good service they will give.

Leger rods

For many years short rods were widely used by leger anglers, but more recently rods with an over-all length of 10 or 11 ft. have become popular and there is little doubt that these longer rods are superior to the shorter ones. For one thing a long rod makes casting far simpler, and for another when a fish does decide to pick up your bait it is easier to drive the hook home with a long rod. For all round legering a hollow glass or split cane carp rod of the type known as the MK IV is ideal. This type of rod was originally designed by Richard Walker, and is in my opinion a masterpiece. Carp rods are made in two sections, and combine not only power, but an easy action which is ideally suited for casting even a light bait a considerable distance.

Spinning rods

A suitable rod for pike and perch spinning can be obtained for a very reasonable price, and nowadays a great many patterns in hollow and solid fibre-glass are on the market. If possible always make sure that you buy a rod of 8 ft. or more in length for the longer the rod the more control you will have over your terminal tackle, and also any fish that you hook. A good spinning rod should have a supple lively action, that runs right down through the cork handle.

Rod rests

Rod rests are an essential part of any keen angler's equipment, and to fish properly you require both a front and a back rest. The back rest consists of a simple Y shape, but the front rest is specially shaped so that the weight of the rod does not trap the line in any way. For fishing in reservoirs or other man-made waters which have concrete banks, a one-piece adjustable rest should be purchased.

COMMON BREAM

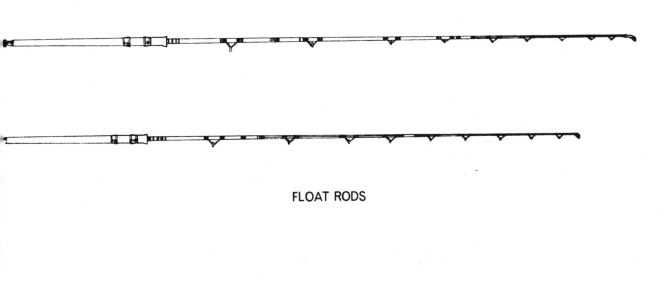

FLOAT RODS

LEGER RODS

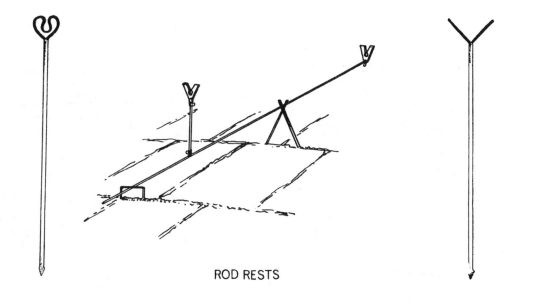

ROD RESTS

Tackle—Reels

Fixed-spool reels

More fixed-spool reels are now used in this country than any other type of reel, for with one of these reels even an amateur can cast easily and quickly. Accuracy, however, can only be achieved through practice. There are numerous well-known brands on the market, ranging in price from 12s. 6d. to over £12. When buying a reel always choose a well-known make. If anything should go wrong spare parts are then always available.

Casting with a fixed-spool reel

Casting with a fixed-spool reel is simple. First open the pick-up of the reel, and hold the line in the crook of the forefinger. Next swing the rod back, then flick it forwards. At the same time straighten the forefinger, which will release the line and allow it to shoot freely from the reel spool.

Centre-pin reels

On fast running rivers the best reel to use for float fishing is a free running centre-pin, for its smoothly machined drum or spool will turn easily to the pull of a well-shotted float, and then long trotting for roach, chub or barbel will become a pleasure.

Casting with a centre-pin

Accurate distance casting with a centre-pin is extremely difficult and will take a considerable number of hours to perfect. It is well worth spending this time, however, for once you have mastered a centre-pin reel casting becomes very simple. A useful method is the F. K. Wallis Avon cast. First, with the left hand draw off two loops of line from between the first and second rod rings. Then keeping the little finger of the right hand on the rim of reel drum, swing the rod back, and then smartly forwards so that the float and trace shoot out in the desired direction. At the same time release the line held by the fingers of the left hand and flick the reel drum with the little finger of the right hand. This sets the reel in motion and the weight of the float and terminal tackle keeps it moving until the required distance is reached. Then the revolving reel drum should be stopped. To start with cast with only a single loop of line held in the left hand. Once you have mastered the method start to practise with two loops.

Method of winding line on to a reel

When you put new line on to a reel spool, make certain that it is wound on as firmly as possible. If it is loose you will have nothing but trouble, for one loop will drop under another and the result will be a dreadful bird's-nest.

The easiest way to wind on line is as follows: First enlist a helper. Next pass a pencil through the hole in the spool of nylon. Then attach the reel to the rod. Pass the end of the nylon through the first rod ring and knot it firmly on to the reel spool or drum. Now the second person should hold the two ends of the pencil firmly so that as you start to turn the reel handle the spool of nylon will revolve steadily to the pull of the reel. In this way the line will feed neatly from the spool on to the reel.

ROACH

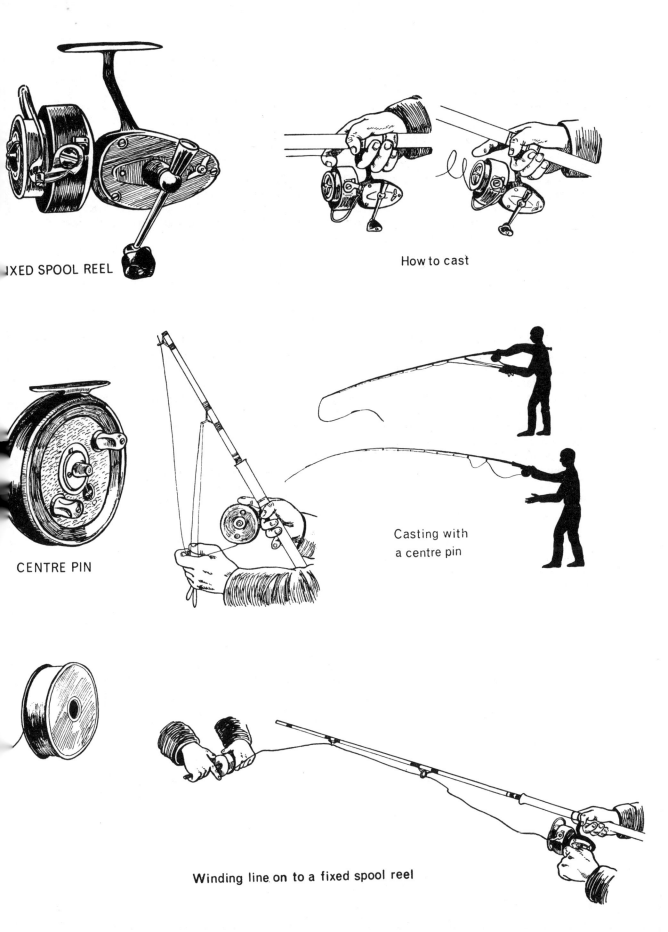

FIXED SPOOL REEL

How to cast

CENTRE PIN

Casting with
a centre pin

Winding line on to a fixed spool reel

Tackle—Floats

Most anglers like to float fish, for there is a subtle fascination in watching the first stirrings of a well-balanced float as a hungry fish noses and nibbles at the carefully prepared bait. Don't, however, make the mistake of thinking that a float is only used as a bite indicator, for this is wrong. The main purpose of the float is to suspend and support the bait at whatever depth the fish happen to be feeding. For this reason it pays to take a lot of trouble when choosing a float for a day's fishing. Don't, for instance, always use the same float for every occasion because each stretch of water you fish will probably need a different size and shape of float. This applies particularly to river fishing where the varying speed of the current has to be judged accurately; otherwise, if the float used is too light or too heavy, the bait will be presented to the fish at the wrong depth.

River floats are generally much heavier than those used in still and slow moving waters. Unfortunately many anglers still believe that any big float will catch fish in rough fast water. This is a fallacy for unless the float is streamlined enough to dip or go under as the hungry fish sucks in the bait, the chances are the fish will feel the resistance and immediately spit the bait out, and possibly go right off the feed for the remainder of the day.

For still or very slow moving waters where there is little or no current to contend with, much lighter floats can be used for most types of fishing. Bird or porcupine quills are the nicest of all still-water floats because being long and evenly tapered, they offer little resistance to a taking fish. Bird quills are easy to get, and can be quickly trimmed down to take only one or two split shot.

Occasionally strong winds will ruffle the surface of the water to such an extent that you will find it difficult to see an ordinary float in the rough water. More important still, as the float bobs up and down with the action of the water the bait will continually rise and fall, and very few fish will be fool enough to take a bait which is behaving in this un-natural manner. There are two ways to overcome this problem. Either you can change tackle completely and use a leger or you can change floats and use an antenna float. These floats are specially designed to overcome the problem of wind ruffled water. The 2nd, 3rd and 4th floats in the middle line opposite are antenna floats.

Anti-wind floats for use in running water are entirely different to those used for still water angling, for instead of having the long thin stem, they have no top at all. Instead the body of the float is rounded off so that the float sits low down in the water.

During the winter months pike fishing is a very popular pastime, and the majority of pike fishermen still use live baits fished on float tackle. Very often the floats these anglers buy and use are far too large even for pike fishing. Admittedly a very buoyant float has to be employed if you intend to use big livebaits but on average it is usually possible to fish with a float which only takes half-an-ounce of lead to make it sit up properly in the water. Although pike have the reputation of being rather stupid and insensitive creatures, this is not true. Consequently it is desirable to use a streamlined float just sufficiently buoyant to support the lead and live bait.

The fourth Pike float illustrated is a French Plastic Float, which can be used either as a fixed or sliding float, simply by retaining or removing the centre stem as required.

CRUCIAN CARP

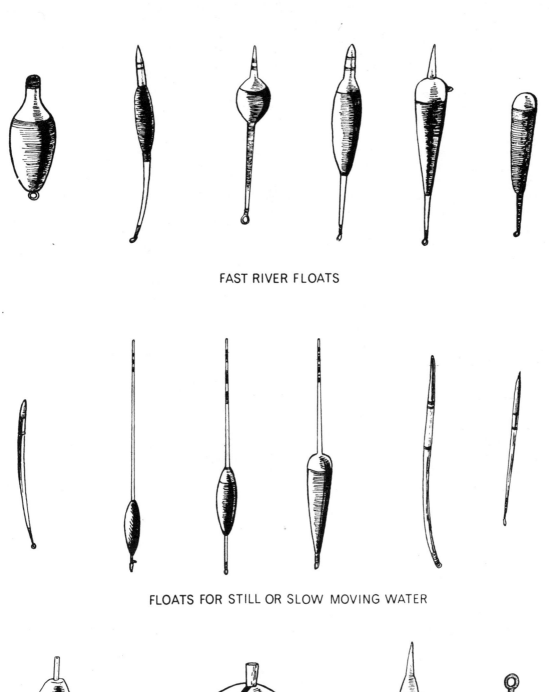

FAST RIVER FLOATS

FLOATS FOR STILL OR SLOW MOVING WATER

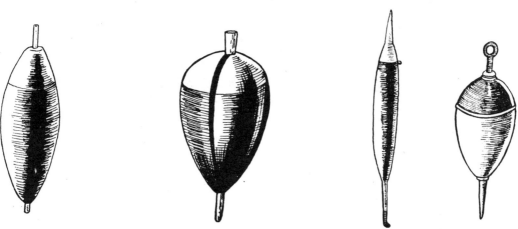

PIKE FLOATS

Tackle—Swivels and Hooks

Swivels are mainly used by pike anglers who employ them for joining nylon lines to steel traces, or traces to artificial baits. Naturally there are many types of swivels available, but for all round use the three most practical swivels are the Barrel Swivel, the Link Swivel, and the Three Way Swivel. These are sold in various sizes. The smaller they are the better, providing you make absolutely certain that the ones you choose are strong enough for the job in hand. Always keep your swivels well oiled and at the slightest sign of rust replace them with new ones. Rust will weaken them considerably, and may cause you to lose a really big fish.

Hooks are legion, and many anglers never bother to buy any special type or shape of hook. Instead they rely on their tackle dealer to supply them with a suitable hook. As far as hooks which are already tied to a nylon cast are concerned this is easy enough to do, but if you prefer to use eyed hooks, then you should choose your hooks carefully.

There are many good patterns available, and Allcocks Model Perfects or Chapmans Gold-strike hooks are as good as any.

A useful hook for worms is the Sealey Bait-holder hook. This has two extra barbs on its shank, which hold the worm firmly in position, even if really long casting is called for.

For pike fishing a treble or double hook is useful. These can be bought either mounted on wire or without the wire.

The size of hook you intend to use depends a great deal on the size of bait you use. For maggots, hempseed or wheat, hooks, from size 12 to 16 are the most useful; for worms, or medium sized pieces of bread paste size 6 to 10 are best; and for large potato or bread baits for carp fishing size 2 or 4 hooks should be used.

For most coarse fish the hooks can be tied directly to the nylon line or to a nylon trace, but for pike it is better to use a wire trace, as the fish may bite through a nylon line.

You can buy pike tackles ready made or you can make up your own with hooks, wire and swivels. This is cheaper and you can vary the length of your traces as you like.

A swivel should always be used to connect wire to nylon, otherwise the wire will quickly cut through the nylon and the first good fish that takes the bait will cause the worn nylon to snap.

Artificial baits of the revolving type often twist and kink the line or trace. To counteract this tendency an anti-kink vane is extremely useful. This acts as a stabilizer and stops line twist. Vanes of this kind can be purchased from any tackle stockist (Bottom diagram).

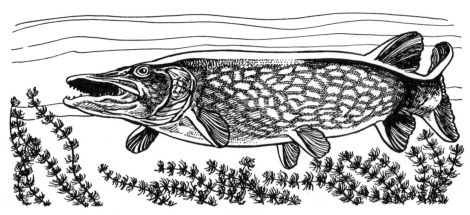

PIKE

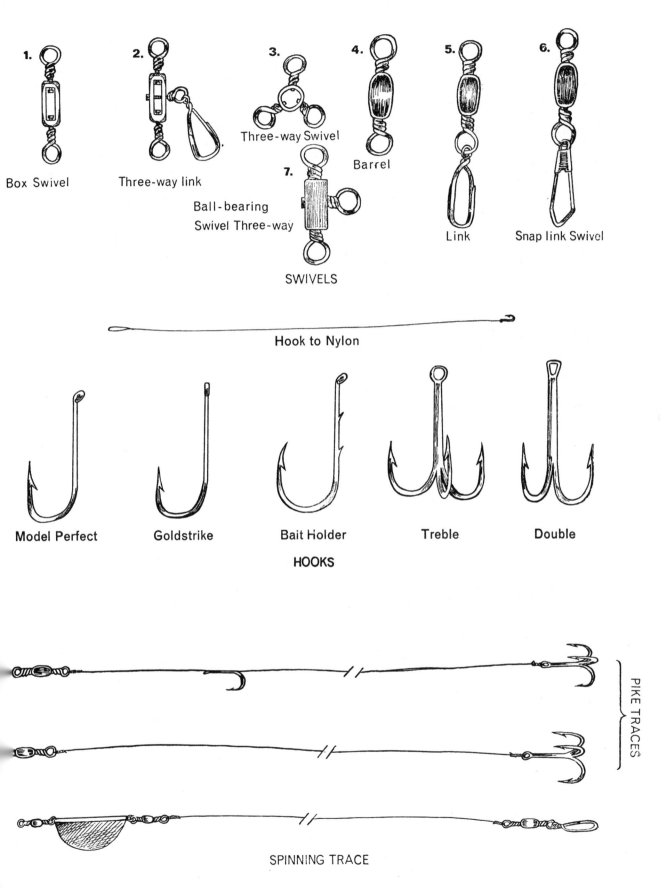

1. Box Swivel

2. Three-way link

3. Three-way Swivel

4. Barrel

5. Link

6. Snap link Swivel

7. Ball-bearing Swivel Three-way

SWIVELS

Hook to Nylon

Model Perfect

Goldstrike

Bait Holder

Treble

Double

HOOKS

PIKE TRACES

SPINNING TRACE

Tackle—Miscellaneous

It is surprising just how many items of tackle the average angler carries about with him on his weekly expedition to the waterside. Much of it he seldom uses but there will always come a day when he needs one or other of these small bits of equipment and unless he has it to hand, a good day's fishing may well be ruined.

Disgorgers are always useful. A disgorger is used only as an implement for removing deep set hooks from a landed fish. It must be used carefully or you may fatally damage your catch.

Pike gags are devised to keep a pike's jaws open while you take out the hooks.

Line winders enable you to carry safely any traces, etc., complete with floats and shot, that you have made up at home. It is a good idea to carry a small winder, or a slotted piece of cardboard, on which to wind any spare pieces of nylon that you cut or break off during fishing. Take them home and burn them. If you throw them away they are a real danger to birds, who get entangled with the stuff and die.

Leger leads come in all shapes and sizes ranging from the expensive bomb-shaped leads which incorporate a built-in swivel, through to the plain old fashioned drilled bullets or coffin-shaped leads.

The most useful weight of lead to buy is half an ounce. This can be used for most leger work, the exception being very fast water; then you may have to double the weight of your lead before you are able to hold bottom.

Split shots are best bought in mixed lots which contain large, medium and small shot. These handy little weights are split so that they can be clamped on to the line below the float.

Small fish can easily be lifted right out of the water but you can't do this with big fish or your line will break. Consequently it is necessary to use a landing net or, in the case of pike, a gaff. A gaff consists of a sharp metal barb-less hook attached to a long metal or wooden handle. This should be used carefully and remember that a pike should only be gaffed through the front end of its lower jaw.

Landing nets are used for all other fish, and if you expect to catch big fish such as carp then make sure that your net is large enough or you may easily lose your best fish.

Keep-nets too should be on the large size, otherwise your fish will be crowded together and many may die as a direct result of this overcrowding. Always make sure that most of the net is sunk as far as possible into the water. This gives the fish more room to move and breathe.

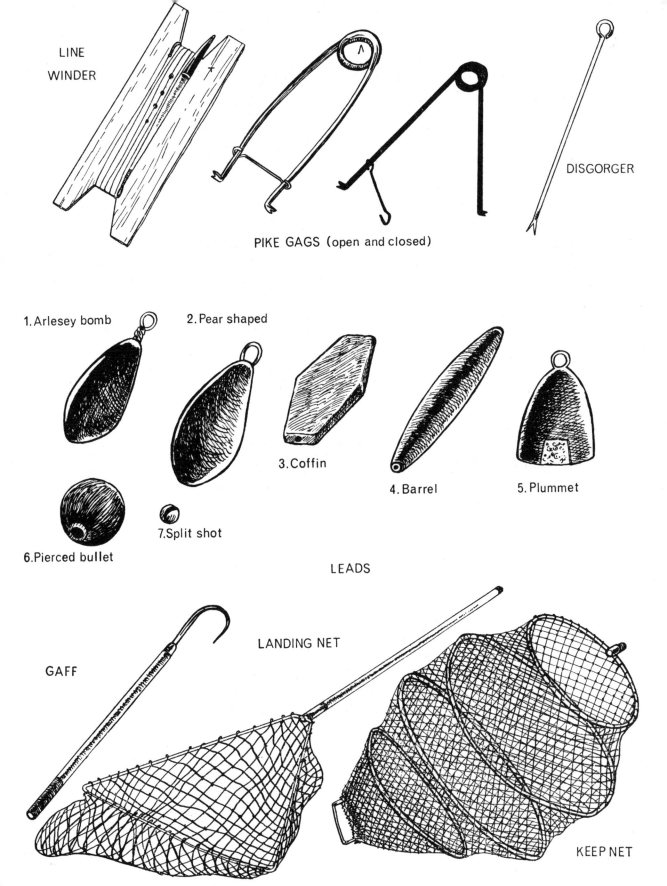

LINE WINDER

PIKE GAGS (open and closed)

DISGORGER

1. Arlesey bomb
2. Pear shaped
3. Coffin
4. Barrel
5. Plummet
6. Pierced bullet
7. Split shot

LEADS

GAFF

LANDING NET

KEEP NET

Knots

The Double Blood Knot

There are a great many knots which can be used by anglers and to describe each in detail would require a great deal of space. The following are those considered most useful for everyday work.

The first is the Double Blood Knot. This is the only really safe method of joining two lengths of nylon together. To tie the knot first place the two ends alongside each other. Now turn the end marked "B" three times round the section marked "A", then insert the end "B" through the space created where the two ends cross. Next twist the end "A" three times round the shaft of "B" and finish by pushing the end "A" through the remaining space. Finally pull the knot tight and cut off the two projecting ends.

The Half Blood Knot

This is used for attaching a swivel or an eyed hook to the line or cast. First thread the end of the line through the eye of the hook or swivel, then twist it four or five times round the main line. Now simply pass the end through the loop of line just above the eye of the hook, etc., and pull the knot tight. Then trim off the short length of waste line as before.

Knot for joining two loops

Many anglers use hooks which are already attached to a nylon hook-length that ends in a loop. This in turn has to be attached to the reel line. The usual method is to tie a small loop in the end of the reel line and then pass the loop of the cast through this. Finally bring the hook up through the loop and pull the two loops tightly together. This gives a neat but strong knot.

The Whipping Knot

A knot for attaching eyed hooks directly to the main reel line, generally confined to large hooks for heavy fishing. As with the Half Blood Knot the loose end of the line should be passed through the eye of the hook. Next bend it back to form a loop. Now with the loose end whip half a dozen turns of line over the loop and the shank of the hook, then pass the end of the line through the free opening of the loop. Pull the knot tight and trim off any surplus line.

If you learn how to tie the four knots just described you will be able to fish with confidence, for you will stand a good chance of successfully landing a monster if and when it comes your way. The finest equipment is useless if your knots will not hold when you hook a big fish.

(a) Knot loosely completed.

(b) Knot pulled tight, with loose ends of line snipped off (Bottom, right).

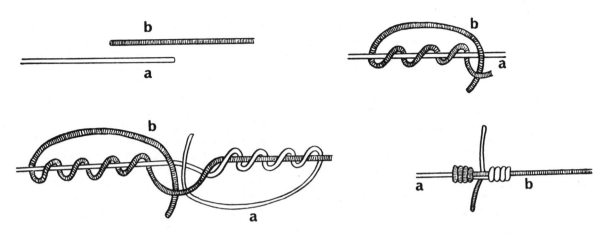

DOUBLE BLOOD KNOT

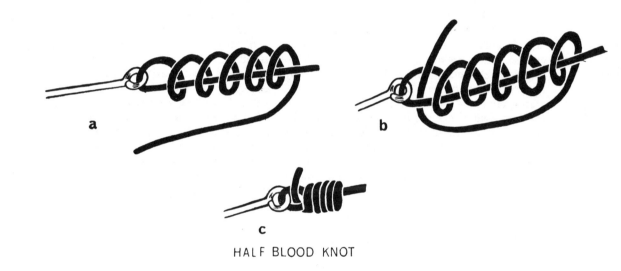

HALF BLOOD KNOT

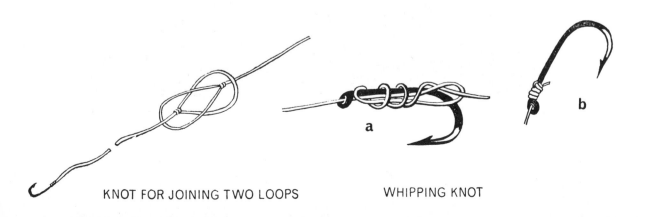

KNOT FOR JOINING TWO LOOPS   WHIPPING KNOT

Baits—1

Almost any edible object can be used as bait to catch fish. On average, however, it pays to stick to the more conventional and well tried lures. Undoubtedly the most popular of these is the gentle or maggot. This is the grub of the common blue-bottle fly. These can be obtained from most tackle shops and for a shilling or two you will be able to purchase enough maggots to last throughout a day's fishing.

In the Midlands and the north of England, however, where match fishing is popular, it is common for anglers to use as many as £2 worth of maggots during the course of a single match. Most of these are thrown in as groundbait.

As a rule maggots are sold in their natural form but match fishermen often dye them in various bright colours. The dyeing process is simple. First the coloured dye is introduced into the bran or sawdust in which the maggots cleanse themselves. The grubs are then allowed to work through it until they absorb the dye and turn the required colour.

Many anglers spoil the attractiveness of a maggot by threading it onto the hook, instead of just nicking the point of the hook through the skin on the grub's square end, which allows it to wriggle freely and so attract the attention of any hungry fish that happens to be in the vicinity. Almost every species of coarse fish can be caught on maggots used either singly or in bunches. The same thing applies to worms, which are without doubt the finest of all natural baits.

There are several kinds of worms but in my experience all of them will catch fish. Big fish, of course, usually prefer large worms but even a big worm can be broken in half, or two or three small worms can be bunched on a hook. So as long as you are able to dig up a supply of worms, irrespective of size, you can fish with absolute confidence.

Bread baits are also very effective particularly for large bottom feeding fish such as carp, bream and tench. Bread paste is particularly good and it can be made up easily at home. Stale bread makes the best paste. This should be mixed with water and kneaded into a pulp or paste. There is an art to paste making, for good bread paste should be stiff enough to stay on the hook and yet soft enough for the hook to penetrate when the strike is made. Very occasionally it may be useful to add colouring to bread paste. Custard powder, for instance, turns the bait yellow. It may possibly succeed in over-fished waters where the fish may be suspicious of white paste.

Flake is another exceptionally good bread bait. Many good catches of carp, tench and chub have been made on it. Flake is simply the white bread from the inside of a new loaf. For carp fishing tear off a lump the size of a golf ball and pinch the bread round the hook shank. It is very important not to squeeze the bread all over for it has a tendency to solidify in water and once this happens it is difficult to pull a hook through it.

Flake is a useful bait in waters that contain a lot of soft bottom weed. Being light it sinks slowly and instead of sinking into the weed it sits gently on top of it, in full view of the fish. To use crust bait simply tear a piece from the outside of an uncut loaf and thread it directly on to the hook.

Small pieces of crust make good roach baits, while lumps the size of a matchbox can be used for carp fishing.

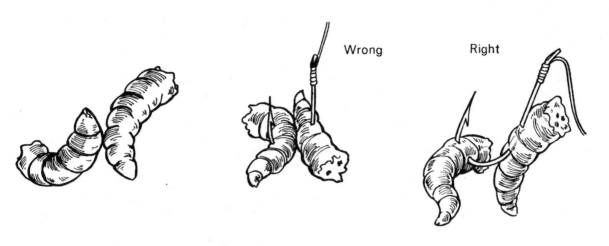

Wrong

Right

MAGGOTS

Wrong and right method of baiting up with maggots

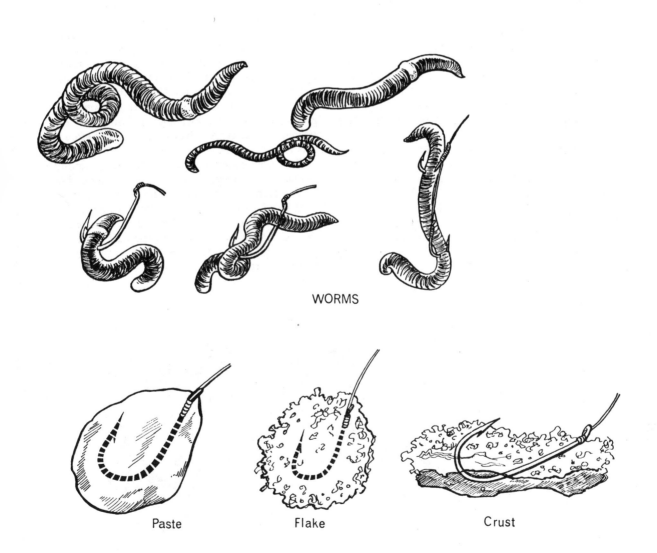

WORMS

Paste

Flake

Crust

BREAD BAITS

Baits—2

Carp fishermen are often troubled by small fish which make a considerable nuisance of themselves by taking bread or worm baits. To overcome this problem many ingenious baits and methods have been tried. Many of them have been successful but perhaps the simplest solution to the small fish problem is to use a small par-boiled potato as bait. Carp quickly learn to feed on potatoes providing you throw a few into the water before actually fishing. Where possible the potatoes should be "new" and boiled just long enough for their skins to dent when pressed between the fingers.

When using potatoes as bait they should be threaded on to the line with a baiting needle. Once the bait is in position, the hook can be tied on and the bait slid back down the line until the hook is almost hidden. Once on the hook the potato should be peeled, leaving only a small patch of skin on each end to cushion the effect of casting.

A favourite bait among roach fishermen is hempseed and on waters where the fish are educated to this bait, it is of little use trying any other baits for roach of all sizes seem to find hempseed irresistible. It is difficult to know just why roach find hemp so attractive. The most popular theory is that the roach take it because they mistake it for very small water snails.

Hempseed can be bought either through a tackle dealer or from a pet shop. To prepare it for the hook it should be soaked for a few hours in water and then simmered gently until each grain starts to split and expose the white pith. It is amazing how fast roach will congregate where hemp is being used as groundbait and for this reason it should only be used in moderation otherwise the fish will gorge themselves on it.

When baiting up with hempseed the bend of the hook should be pushed into the split in the seed and not right through the husk. Always groundbait sparingly and a good tip is to throw a few grains into the swim every time a fish is hooked. This will then stop the remainder of the shoal from breaking up.

Stewed wheat is another good bait which sometimes succeeds when all other baits have failed. Wheat should be cooked in the same way as hemp, or as an added attraction it can be cooked in milk. This keeps the wheat white in colour for it has a tendency to darken when stewed in water.

An easy way to prepare the bait is to put it into a vacuum flask and then top up the flask with boiling liquid and leave it corked up overnight. It will then be ready to use as bait in the morning. Hempseed or wheat can be kept in a bait tin but a linen bag is better.

Groundbait is used to attract fish to the actual hookbait and where possible you should try to attract but not feed the fish. This, of course, is not always possible. Bran makes the best base for a groundbait mixture, for by adding or subtracting water you can make it thick or thin at will. For still water the mixture should be thin so that it spreads out in a cloud round the hookbait. In fast water the groundbait has to be thick and solid otherwise the strength of the current will wash it away before it gets to the bottom.

To make groundbait more attractive a handful of maggots or chopped worms can be added. For rudd which are a surface feeding fish, a slice of oven dried bread tied to a weighted string is a useful form of groundbait and on carp waters where the fish are known to feed on the surface, a few pieces of loose crust scattered about on the surface will often attract a fish or two.

RUDD

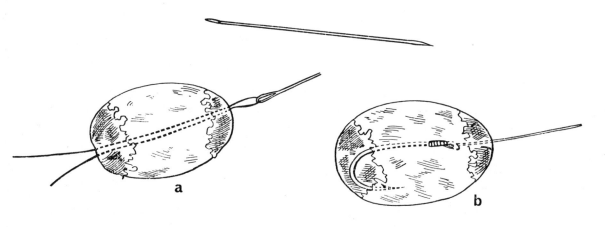

How to bait up with par-boiled potato

HEMPSEED

WHEAT

LINEN BAG

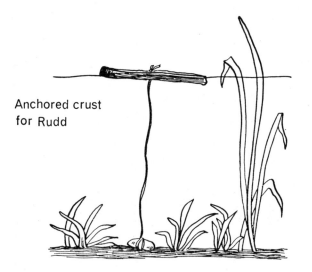

Anchored crust for Rudd

GROUNDBAIT

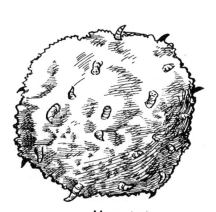

Maggots in a ball of bran

Predatory fish such as pike and perch are naturally attracted by live fish baits and for both species livebaiting is still the most popular method. Almost any small fish can be employed as bait and big pike have been caught on small pike and perch on perch. Normally, only small fish are used as livebait and for general pike fishing a 6 or 8 in. roach is quite sufficient. If, however, you are lucky enough to locate an exceptionally large pike, then it may well pay to use a very big livebait.

Dennis Pye, of Norwich, who has probably caught more pike over 20 lb. than any other living angler, often uses roach and bream weighing a pound or more as bait. Mind you, it does not always follow that you will catch big fish on big baits but generally speaking if you do get a bite while using a large livebait, the chances are a pike of at least 10 lb. is responsible.

There are many ways of hooking a livebait and for small or medium sized baits I find that a single treble hook (top left) through the lip of the bait is quite adequate but for big baits something more substantial is called for and it pays to use a two hook snap tackle (top right). These are known as Jardine tackles and are stocked by most tackle shops.

There is no doubt that impaling a live fish on a big hook is an unpleasant business and for those anglers who cannot bring themselves to do this, a legered deadbait is the obvious answer. Dead baiting as such is a recent introduction and it is mainly due to Fred J. Taylor and his two brothers that this method has gained popularity. Extensive experiments by these three famous anglers have shown that pike, particularly big ones, become lazy and lethargic and whenever possible they like to pick up dead or dying fish rather than hunt down active fish. Nowadays, many of the big pike which are reported in the angling press are caught on deadbaits and nearly always the successful bait is legered herring. It is not known why pike prefer a sea fish to a fresh water fish but the fact remains that they do and experiments with two rods, one baited with a dead roach or dace and another with herring, show that most of the bites have been registered by the herrings rod. This, of course, is very handy, for herrings can always be bought from a wet fish shop and a pound or two will last for a day's fishing.

Pike also respond to groundbait, in the form of chopped herring or whole sprats.

A herring makes a heavy bait and naturally enough it pays to use substantial tackle for deadbaiting. The trace in particular should be made up with two trebles and a single hook. The bait is mounted so that it hangs head down and each hook helps to support the weight. In rough windy conditions herrings can be fished on straightforward pike float tackle, for the action of the wind-whipped waves will cause the float to bob up and down and impart a little life to the bait.

Big eels feed a great deal on small fish and one of the finest of all eel baits is a small dead fish. Shiny fish like roach, dace or bleak seem to make the best eel baits but if these are unobtainable then almost any small fish can be employed. Big eels are very shy and cautious feeders and if they feel anything hard or unnatural about a bait they will quickly spit it out. For this reason it pays to use only one large single hook. The line should be threaded right through the deadbait with a baiting needle. Then the hook should be tied on and pulled back into the bait's mouth so that only the point and barb projects. Small split shot should then be pinched on to the line close to the tail of the bait. This will stop it from sliding back up the line.

When using fresh fish baits always make sure that the swim bladder is pierced otherwise the bait will float up from the bottom and catch nothing.

EEL

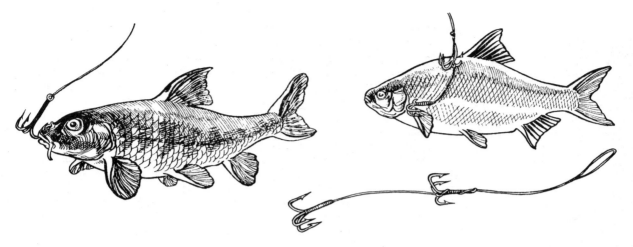

Two methods of baiting up with livebait

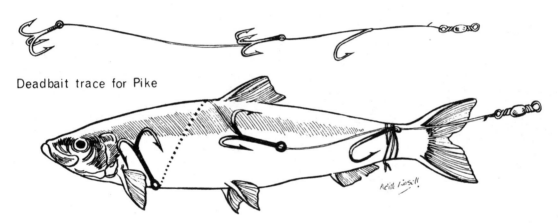

Deadbait trace for Pike

Mounted deadbait

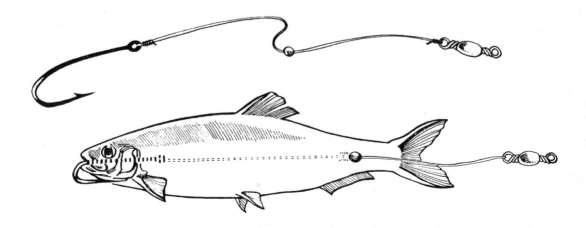

Deadbait for eels

The freshwater crayfish (a) is a bait for big chub. At one time this bait was used only on the Great Ouse but nowadays it is used extensively throughout the British Isles wherever chub and crayfish are found together.

Crayfish are found only in clean water and as a rule they live mainly where the stream or river runs through clay, for here they burrow into the soft soil, and providing you are careful, you can extract them from their holes by hand.

Crayfish are also attracted by dead fish and an easy way to catch a supply of crayfish for bait is to tie a fish or piece of fish into the mesh of a landing net (b), sink it in a suitable place and lift it at regular intervals to remove any crayfish that happen to be feeding on the fish bait. Crayfish can be used whole on leadless, floatless tackle and as a rule chub take them very boldly providing, of course, that they do not become alarmed beforehand (c).

In recent years, many people have taken to spending their holidays either camping beside or boating upon rivers. Naturally enough, much of their waste food finds its way into the water. In consequence, several new baits have been discovered, the most prominent of which has been sausage which is now used extensively by both barbel and chub anglers. Sausages can be used either raw or cooked. On the Thames this bait is particularly good.

The correct way to use an uncooked sausage is to snip off both ends and hook it through once. This enables the barbel to pick up the bait and suck out part of the inside. This gives the fish confidence and as a rule it will then take the rest of the sausage into its mouth.

If you prefer a more substantial bait, boil or grill the sausage and cut it up into bait-sized chunks. Whichever way you decide to use sausage bait, always bear in mind that it is at best a soft bait so always strike at the slightest indication of a bite. If you delay the strike the fish will suck the bait off the hook and depart with a free meal.

During the early part of the season when the fish are still in the faster water after their spawning activities, silkweed can be a deadly bait. Silkweed is actually a soft weed which grows on the piles of weirs and lock gates. Its soft fronds give shelter to all sorts of minute aquatic insects and it is these that the fish are attracted to.

To use silkweed as bait it should never be handled. Instead, the hook should be pulled through the growing weed until it picks up a suitable portion. Bites on silkweed are usually very decisive and very few fish will be missed. Although it is only normally looked upon as a roach bait, silkweed is also good for barbel and chub fishing.

Minnows make first-class livebaits and when dead they can be used for spinning for perch and pike. Although minnows are usually found in dense shoals, rod fishing is not a profitable method of obtaining them for bait and if you require minnows in any quantity a plastic minnow trap (from your tackle stockist) is the best thing to use. This trap consists of a tube with a funnel type entrance at both ends. A few crumbs of bread are all that are needed to draw the little fish into the tube. Half an hour spent with a trap will usually produce enough minnows for a day's fishing.

CHUB

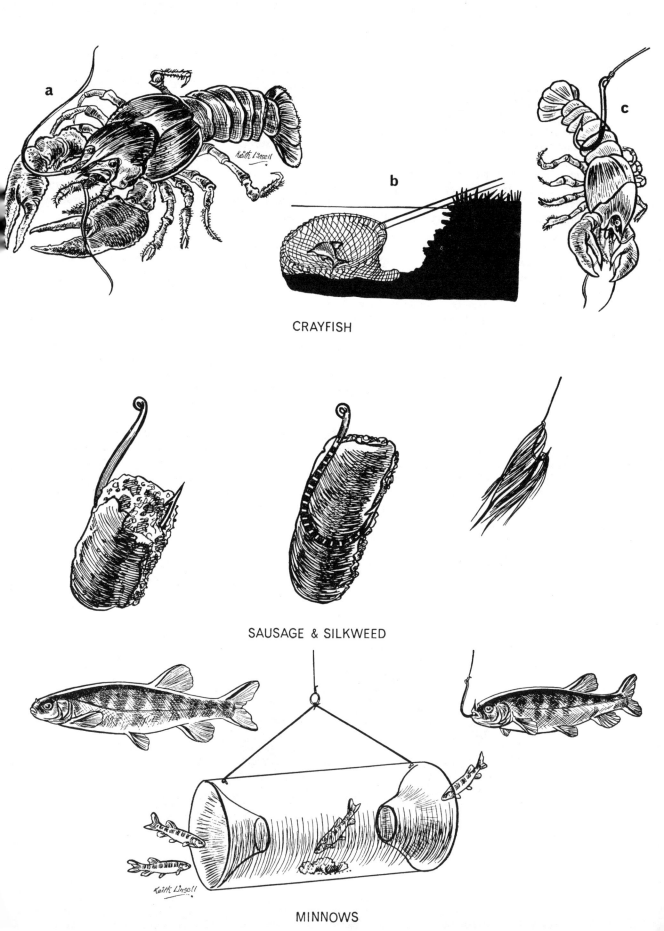

CRAYFISH

SAUSAGE & SILKWEED

MINNOWS

Float Fishing—1

Float fishing is a very popular and effective way of catching fish and a great many anglers prefer it to all other forms of angling.

Generally speaking, the average size of fish caught on float tackle is smaller than that of leger-caught fish but to make up for this you will usually catch more fish on float-fished baits than on legered ones. If you are able to judge the various conditions and change from one style to another as these conditions change, then you will be able to consistently catch fish.

Where the water is still or very slow moving, it is often possible to combine float fishing with light legering. This method is known as "laying on" and is a great favourite among roach fishermen. The term to "lay on" means exactly what it says. First the exact depth of the water is ascertained, then the float is pushed up the line about another 18 in. so that most of the split shot and a foot or so of line lie on the bottom. When the tackle is set properly, the float will half cock on the surface. Bites are clearly indicated by the float which will either bob once or twice and disappear beneath the surface, or rise out of the water and lie flat before moving away.

If the water is too deep for normal float fishing, a sliding float can be employed. This moves freely on the line and is stopped at the required distance from the hook by a tiny piece of rubber band which is tied directly to the reel line.

A very delicate form of the laying on technique is the lift method which was devised by Fred J. Taylor who is known throughout the angling world for his catches of large fish. Originally, the lift method was designed for tench fishing but it can be used for other species as well.

Lift tackle is very simple to arrange. First a tiny float, preferably a small bird or porcupine quill should be attached to the line by the bottom end only. Then a single split shot should be clipped on to the line, 1 or at most 1½ in. from the hook. The float should then be set so that it sits bolt upright on the surface, which means that there must be no slack line between the float and the split shot. Bites are registered by the float keeling over on to the surface as the fish picks up the bait and lifts the single shot from the bottom. It is essential to strike as soon as the float starts to move, otherwise you may easily miss the fish completely.

Long trotting is a technique that is only used on faster rivers but under the right conditions it can be very deadly indeed. To get the best out of this method it is necessary to choose your swim very carefully. The ideal swim to look for is one that starts off as a fast glide and gradually deepens into a run 10 to 12 yards long. If this run is surrounded on both sides by beds of thick bottom weed, all the better, for fish like to feed close to cover.

Having found this type of swim, the angler should station himself 15 to 20 yards upstream and begin operations. The float is set so that the bait drags along the bottom and the pull of the current on the large float should be sufficient to "trot" the bait steadily downstream. Once the tackle is underway, the float should be checked very slightly with the rod tip so that the shot and baited hook precede it. Generally, the tackle should be allowed to move fairly freely with the current so that the bait can appear naturally to the waiting fish. At the end of the swim, however, it often pays to check the float firmly so that the force of the water lifts the bait right up off the bottom. This trick will often catch the larger fish in the swim.

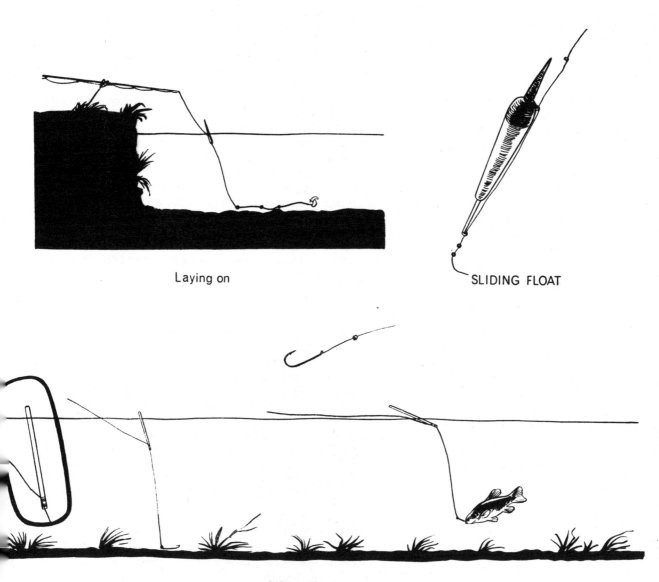

Laying on

SLIDING FLOAT

Lift method

Long trotting.

Float Fishing—2

On warm summer evenings when the water temperature is high, roach and rudd often rise to the surface to feed on minute insects and other edible objects. Fish feeding in this manner often give away their whereabouts by splashing and rolling right on the surface and once you have located a shoal of fish that are feeding in this manner it is usually fairly easy to catch several before the shoal finally moves away in search of a fresh feeding area.

Obviously, if the fish are feeding on the surface, it is pointless to set up the tackle so that the bait hangs close to the bottom (top left). Consequently, you can do one of two things. Either you can set the float so that it is only 3 or 4 in. from the hook, or better still you can employ slow sinking float tackle. For this you will require a self cocking float, i.e. a float which either contains enough weight to cock it, or a float with a twist of lead wire wrapped round its bottom. On no account must you have any weight on the actual line. With this sort of tackle I usually set the float 12 to 18 in. from the hook. This gives the bait plenty of leeway to sink in a slow and natural manner. Almost any bait can be used on this sort of set up but maggots or bread flake are probably best.

As a rule the fish that fall to these tactics are of a large average size. Bites are very easy to detect with this tackle and normally the float will glide away across the surface in a most determined fashion.

Shallow ponds and broads often contain a vast amount of bottom weed which can make fishing very difficult, for if a bait settles on the weed, the weight of the shot or lead on the line will cause it to sink right into the weed, which will then close over it and hide it from sight. To overcome this problem it is necessary to employ special techniques which although complicated to look at, are simple to use. The most effective of these is the light float paternoster. This, as the diagram shows, has a long link between the reel line and the hook. To fish this kind of tackle correctly, accurate plumbing is essential so that the lead goes straight down to the bottom, allowing the bait to fall gently on to the blanket of the weed. Another useful method which I have used while rudd fishing on the Norfolk Broads is also illustrated. This method, however, can only be used with a bread crust bait, for to work properly it relies entirely on the buoyancy of the crust to lift the hook above the thick weed beds. Bites on this type of tackle are usually quite delicate but definite affairs and providing you are watching the float carefully, you should miss very few fish.

Often it is necessary to change floats two or three times during the course of a day's fishing. This can be a fiddley business unless you use a method which consists simply of two float caps which slide freely on the line. The float is then slipped into these and if a change of colour or size of float is called for, the old float can be quickly removed and a new one slipped into position. Split shot can then be added or subtracted depending on the size of the float you have changed to.

BARBEL

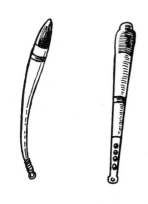

SELF COCKING FLOATS

Slow sinking bait

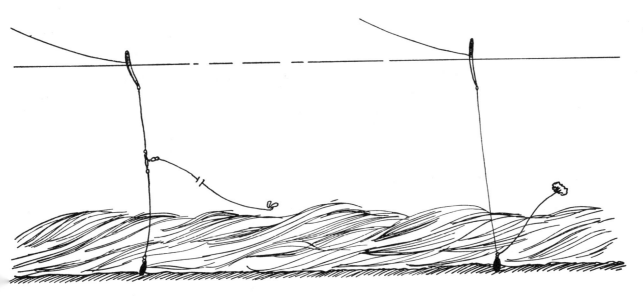

Two methods of overcoming Blanket Weed

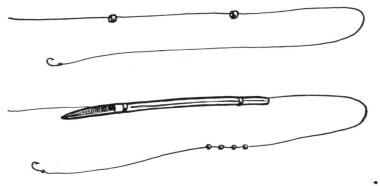

Quick method of changing floats

Float Fishing—3

Float fishing for pike is a fascinating occupation for there is something extremely pleasant about watching a large orange or red float suddenly disappear from view. On open lakes or rivers where there is little or no weed or snags, the tackle can be made up in the same way as normal float tackle, the only difference being that the line is much stronger, the lead much larger and the hook is attached to a wire trace. In weedy waters, however, this sort of tackle cannot really be used for the livebait has a habit of making for the nearest patch of weed, where it quickly snags up the tackle. To overcome this problem the most appropriate rig to use is the float paternoster. This method works well in weedy conditions, for it allows the bait to swim about quite a lot, yet still keeps it from becoming entangled in the surrounding weed. This tackle can also be used in fast water, particularly when you want to keep the bait in a known pike lie.

A three-way swivel is invaluable as a means of joining the hook trace to the main tackle. In very weedy conditions the trace between the lead and the swivel can be of a lighter breaking strain than the reel line, so that if the lead becomes fouled up on some underwater obstruction, you will only lose the lead if you are forced to break the tackle free. This tip can save you a considerable amount of money and is well worth remembering.

When a pike does take the bait, the bite usually follows a set pattern. First, the float will dip and disappear. At this stage you must be prepared to give the taking fish as much free line as it wants, otherwise it will feel the drag of the rod tip and quickly eject the bait and depart. As a rule the fish will take 5 to 10 yards of line on this first run, then it will stop to swallow the bait. As soon as it starts to move away for the second time, you must strike and do not hesitate too long or the fish will gorge the bait and the hooks with it. If this happens the fish will have to be killed. By timing the strike correctly, however, it is usually possible to hook the fish in the corner of its mouth. This will give a firm hold and yet do no damage to the gills or throat of the pike.

During periods of warm weather many river fish have a tendency to gather under the branches of overhanging trees or bushes. They do this for two reasons. One is that they like the shade and the other is that they know that caterpillars and other insects will drop from the leaves into the water and provide them with an easy meal. Chub are particularly fond of tucking themselves away in this sort of place and providing you have the patience and the caution you can often catch one or two very big fish by dapping a live insect bait over their heads. Although dapping is an art, it is not an over-difficult one and providing you can approach the swim quietly enough in the first place, it is simple enough to lower the bait down slowly until it just touches the surface. Often the chub see the bait while it is still well above their heads. If this happens they usually become very excited and often roll about just under the surface in anticipation of a free meal. When you first see the fish behave in this way it is easy to become over-excited and make a hasty movement which will frighten the fish. To avoid this mistake it is essential to remain as calm as possible throughout the operation. Many anglers make the mistake of striking as soon as the bait disappears. It pays to wait until the fish turns down and away before driving the hook home.

Float Paternoster for Pike

Normal Pike tackle

DAPPING

Float Fishing—4

Any angler who has ever had the opportunity of visiting a good carp water during the late evening or early morning must have heard carp sucking or "clooping" on the surface. Often the fish can be heard quite close to the bank and over the years a method of fishing has been devised especially for catching these particular fish.

This method which is known as "margin fishing" was originated by Mr. Richard Walker and other members of the Carp Catchers' Club. Margin fishing is a method which calls for great patience but the result is usually worth while for carp, particularly large ones, have a habit of patrolling the water close to the bank. This is not an aimless occupation by any means for the fish have learned that large amounts of edible matter collect in such places and they simply wander round sucking in all the odd bits of waste bread or other food that they happen to find. Big carp seem to have regular beats and unless they are disturbed or frightened in any way, they can usually be relied upon to visit a swim night after night.

By throwing a few bits of loose crust into the water for two or three nights in a row, you can even encourage the fish to search for food in a particular swim and once this happens it is easy enough to get the fish to accept a bait providing, of course, you are able to sit perfectly still for hours on end. If you so much as move your feet you will almost certainly frighten the fish and if this happens you may be sure that that particular carp will not return for the remainder of the night.

Crust fishing on a long range basis is also an effective and very exciting method of catching carp. Normally weedy waters are best suited to crust fishing techniques and a bait cast out close to thick beds of surface weed is more likely to be accepted than a bait cast out into clear water. If you are fishing close to weed it is essential to use a line with a breaking strain of at least 12 lb., for as soon as you strike at a taking fish you must try and pull it away from the weed or it will snag up your tackle and escape. Light lines just will not stand up to these strong arm tactics and although you might be lucky enough to land a big fish with a light line, it does not pay to chance it.

On very warm days carp will often rise to the surface and lie basking in the warmth of the sun. Under these conditions they will usually ignore a bait presented in a conventional manner but they can be caught if you are prepared to take a little trouble and stalk each fish individually.

Stalking a carp is a very tricky business for these fish are ultra-sensitive to heavy footfalls and the slightest vibration is usually enough to send them racing away for shelter. If you are careful you can get to within easy casting range of the fish and then you may well be lucky. Do not make the mistake of casting the bait directly on to the fish for the splash will thoroughly frighten it. Instead, cast the crust out so that it drops 2 or 3 ft. beyond the basking fish and then pull it back until it floats within inches of the carp's mouth. Use a small piece, and to make casting easier give the crust a quick dip in the water before making the cast.

MIRROR & COMMON CARP

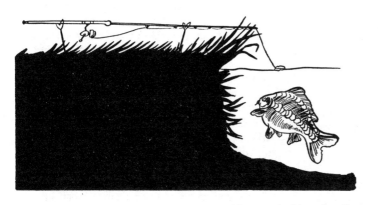

Margin fishing for Carp

Floating crust

Stalking Carp with crust bait

Legering—1

The leger is undoubtedly the best method to use for catching very big fish and the majority of the well-known specimen hunters in this country use various types of leger tackle in preference to the more conventional float fishing techniques.

Unfortunately, legering is a much slower style of angling and for this reason few anglers trouble to learn the various techniques that have to be employed before you are able to consistently catch fish.

In still waters the leger lead should be as small as possible and one of $\frac{1}{2}$ oz. in weight is sufficient except for abnormally long casts.

For running water, of course, the actual weight of the lead you need depends entirely on the strength of the current. In times of flood, for instance, when the river is running bank high, you may well have to use a lead weighing an ounce or more, but under normal conditions a weight of between half and three-quarters of an ounce will be quite sufficient. Normally a leger weight should be heavy enough to hold the bottom but occasionally you may want the weight to roll about a bit. This is a specialized technique described at length in this chapter.

The distance between the lead and the hook depends entirely on the water conditions and the way the fish are feeding. Only experience can show just what is required but to start with it is suggested that you stop the lead 10 or 12 in. from the hook. A small split shot nipped on the line at the required distance makes a good stop.

For extra light work a loop of nylon line holding three or four large swan shots makes a handy weight. The beauty of this tackle is that you can add or subtract a shot or two as and when you need to.

Many carp anglers use the "weightless leger". This simply means that the hook is tied directly to the reel line and there is no lead at all, the weight of the large paste or potato bait being sufficient for casting purposes.

On this kind of tackle bites are registered in a variety of ways, the commonest being the straightforward "run". This is also the easiest to connect with, for the fish simply picks up the bait and races away with it. The slack line bite, on the other hand, is not so easy to strike at, for instead of picking up the bait and moving off with it, the fish will swim in towards the bank. This causes the line between the rod top and the water to fall slack. Unless you can reel in until you feel the fish moving and strike as soon as you make contact, the chances are you will lose the carp.

As most carp fishing is done at night many anglers use an electric bite indicator. These are built into a rod rest and work from a small battery. The line slips behind an antenna on the buzzer head and as the fish moves off with the bait the pull on the line moves the antenna over and makes contact. This in turn sets the buzzer off and warns you that you have a bite. Buzzer indicators of this type can be purchased from any tackle stockist.

Always remember that carp are ultra sensitive creatures that will drop a bait if they feel the slightest check to their movements. Consequently, you must always leave the pick-up of the reel in the open position. If you use a centre-pin reel you should always coil a few yards of line on to a groundsheet so that the fish can run freely with the bait.

As a general rule it pays to fish directly into the wind when legering on still waters. Often this makes it difficult to detect bites. To overcome this problem it helps if you point the rod tip down until it almost touches the surface of the water. Fishing into a strong wind is often difficult and unpleasant but it pays, for the wind pushes along the surface water until it reaches the bank and turns back. The wind-cooled water then sinks and takes down all manner of food. Naturally, the fish know this and congregate in these cooled and naturally groundbaited areas.

Keith Linsell

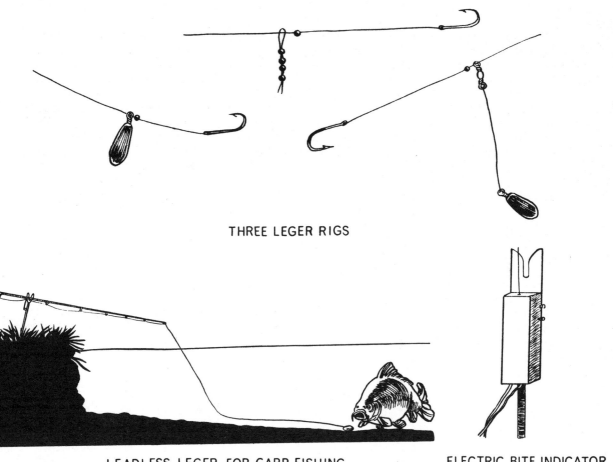

THREE LEGER RIGS

LEADLESS LEGER FOR CARP FISHING

ELECTRIC BITE INDICATOR

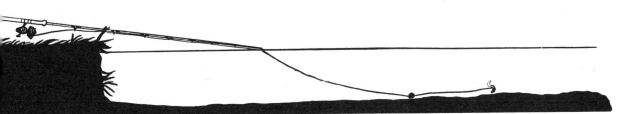

Rod tip pointing down to overcome wind

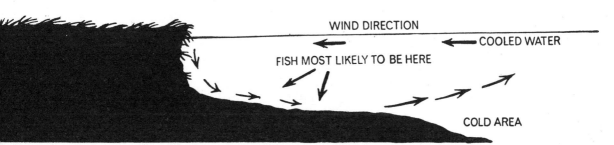

WIND DIRECTION

COOLED WATER

FISH MOST LIKELY TO BE HERE

COLD AREA

Arrows indicate most likely feeding ground

Legering—2

It is never easy to tell whether or not you have a bite while legering, for the fish seldom take the bait in the same way twice. Barbel, for instance, barely make the rod tip dip on one occasion, while on the next trip they may well take the bait so decisively that the rod whips round in a half circle. Many types of bite indicators have been devised by leger fishermen. The commonest of these are the "dough bobbin" and the silver paper indicators which are widely used by still water anglers.

A blob of bread paste or a fold of silver paper is attached to the line either between the reel and the first ring or to the line directly in front of the rod tip. Naturally, the weight of this indicator causes the line to sag down and the slightest pull from a feeding fish will cause the indicator to jump slightly, so warning you that a fish is at the bait. Normally, this type of indicator jumps up two or three times and then slides steadily upwards as the fish takes the bait and moves steadily off. The strike should be made just before the line is actually pulled tight. Timing this to perfection takes time but once you have the knack of it you will rarely miss a definite bite.

An even more sensitive method is to let the line droop freely between the rod tip and the water. This method, however, requires great concentration and is only really practical on windless days. It is, however, amazingly sensitive and providing you have the patience to sit for hours on end watching the line where it enters the water, you will be able to see the slightest flicker of a bite.

Match fishermen have invented and perfected a new type of bite indicator—the swing tip—which is extremely sensitive. It consists of a short, flexible extension of the rod beyond the end ring. It has gained a firm hold among Midland and northern matchmen, but it complicates casting and is not a gadget the beginner need worry about.

A good bite indicator which will work under practically any conditions is constructed from a lady's hairgrip and an ordinary bottle cork. This is attached to a length of string and a skewer. The skewer is stuck firmly into the ground so that when you strike the cork will come off the line but will not vanish for ever in the process.

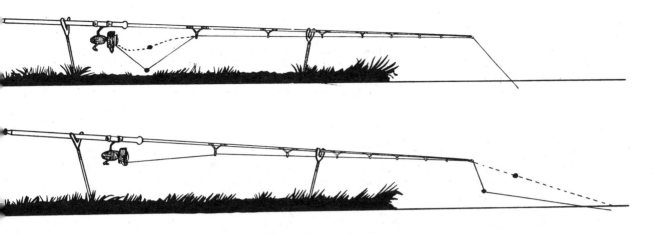

Two methods of bite indication

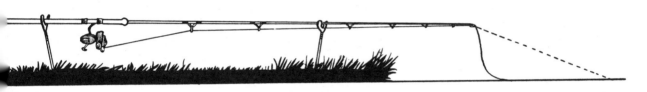

Slack line method

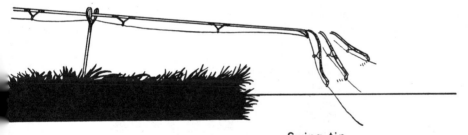

Swing tip

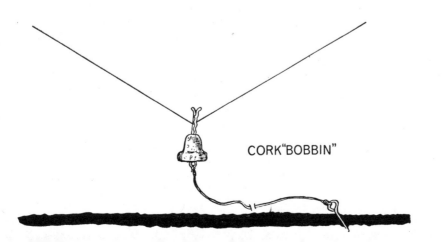

CORK "BOBBIN"

Legering—3

The paternoster is a sort of cross between leger and float tackle and is very useful in deep water reservoirs, lakes or rivers, particularly for perch and pike fishing. Normally, the lead itself is tied directly to the end of the line, while the hook is attached to a 6-in. length of nylon which has a swivel tied to the other end. This slides freely on the line and is stopped at a distance of about 15 in. from the lead by a single split shot. Normally only one hook is used but some anglers use two, one set well above the other and each carrying a different bait. Objections to this idea are that it is quite possible to hook two good fish at once and then lose both of them in the struggle. Even if you only hook one fish at a time the loose hook is likely to become snagged on some underwater obstruction.

Pike fishermen often use a wire paternoster arm to hold the bait well clear of the reel line. This is quite a good idea for livebaits have a habit of twisting about round the line and causing a nasty tangle.

A good method for carp fishing is the suspended crust. This rig is set up in the same way as standard leger tackle, the only difference being that the lead should be set so that the bait will rise to around the mid-water mark. This means that in water 6 ft. deep the distance between the lead and the hook should be approximately 3 ft. To work properly this method relies entirely on the buoyancy of the crust bait, consequently the crust should be large enough to lift the line between the lead and the hook but not buoyant enough to shift the weight from the bottom.

Dead baits for pike are usually legered. Generally speaking pike pick up a dead bait crosswise in their jaws. Then they move off steadily for 5 or 10 yards. During this early stage you must always allow the fish to take line freely. Once it is satisfied that the bait is dead and safe to eat the fish will stop. At this point it turns the bait in its mouth and begins to swallow it head first. As soon as the bait starts to slide down its throat, the pike will usually start to move off again. As soon as this second run is under way the strike should be made.

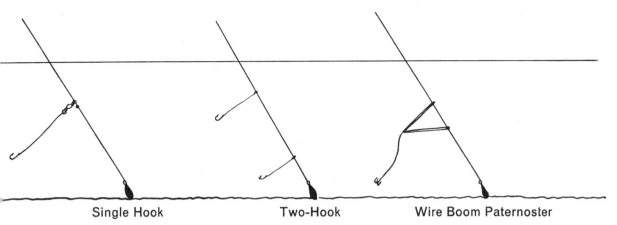

Single Hook   Two-Hook   Wire Boom Paternoster

Three sets of Paternoster tackle

Suspended crust

How a Pike picks up and swallows a deadbait

Legering—4

Many river fishermen use a gadget called a swim feeder when legering. This is a useful appliance, particularly for roach and bream fishing. It consists of a perforated plastic tube fitted with a lead keel to hold it upright on the bottom. Normally, swim feeders are sold with a nylon loop already to attach to the reel line. A small link swivel added to this loop so that the reel line runs through the swivel eye allows the feeder to run freely on the line and makes it much easier to stop at the required distance from the hook.

In use the swim feeder acts both as a ground bait container and a leger lead. The idea being that the tube is packed with groundbait. This gradually seeps out as the feeder lies on the bottom and naturally attracts fish to the area surrounding the baited hook. In still or slow moving water it is a good idea to put a wad of wet groundbait into one end of the feeder, fill up the middle with dry groundbait and then pack the remaining end with more damp bran. This makes a sort of groundbait bomb which explodes a few seconds after reaching the bottom and fills the water in the surrounding area with a cloud of floating bait particles which attract fish to the area very quickly. As the swim feeder also acts as a weight and slides freely on the line, you can use any of the conventional bite indicators already described.

Many still waters have a dense covering of thick soft bottom weed into which a bait presented on standard leger tackle immediately sinks from view. There are several ways of overcoming this problem, one of the simplest and most efficient of which is the wooden leger. This method was devised originally by the late Avon fisherman, Mr. W. Parker, whose catches of monster roach have seldom if ever been equalled.

Originally, the wooden leger was designed solely for roach fishing but it works just as well for other species. The principle is simple. The weight itself consists of a section of drilled dowling rod. This is stopped at either end by a split shot pinched on to the reel line. The weight of these shots should just make the wooden weight sink slowly so that it comes to rest softly on top of the weed. The baited hook drifts down with it and also comes to rest where the fish can see it. Being practically buoyant the wooden leger offers very little resistance to a taking fish.

A similar problem arises in lakes whose bottoms consist of deep soft mud, for a standard leger will quickly sink into this and drag the bait down with it. Frank Guttfield of the Hertfordshire Specimen Hunters Group devised an ingenious set of tackle to overcome this problem. This consists of a thin plastic tube which is attached to the lead by means of a nylon or light wire trace, then another swivel is added so that although the lead may sink into the mud the swivel eye is still held up off the bottom so that the bait rests on top of the mud. Being above the level of the bottom the swivel eye does not become clogged by mud and will turn easily to allow a taking fish to move off in any direction it wants to go. The length of the plastic tube depends, of course, upon the depth of the mud. Only local experience can show what is required for each individual lake or pond.

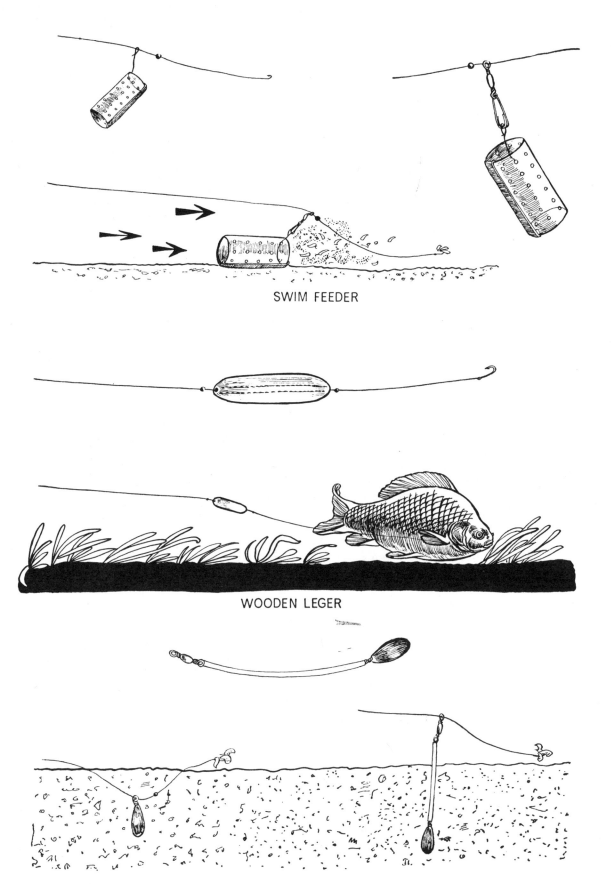

SWIM FEEDER

WOODEN LEGER

Tube lead used to overcome mud

Legering—5

In fast water, particularly where the river is rather shallow, it is easy to frighten the shoals of feeding fish by casting a leger weight directly at them and it pays to use a method of angling known as the rolling leger.

This style of angling originated on the middle and upper reaches of the Thames where it was first used for bream fishing. Since then anglers have discovered that it works equally well for other river fish and on the famous Royalty Fishery at Christchurch, in Hampshire, many of the dedicated anglers who specialize in catching huge barbel and monster chub, use this method more than any other style of legering.

When fishing with a rolling leger you must use a weight which barely holds the bottom. If it sits in one place it is too heavy, for this method relies on the current to shift and roll the weight and bait down to the waiting fish. Always make sure also that you sit on the bank well above the known feeding grounds of the fish, then cast the bait straight out in front of you and let the current roll the tackle round and down to the fish. In this way the bait will be presented in a natural manner. By lengthening or shortening each cast you can thoroughly search out a swim. Always make sure that you hold the rod all the time, for a bite can come from almost any part of the swim and if you are not ready to strike at the slightest sign of a pull on the rod tip, you will miss most of the bites.

To be a good river fisherman it is essential to be able to read the river like a book for unless you know where fish live you will be unable to catch much at all. Most expert anglers are said by many to use a secret bait. This, of course, is nonsense and the real secret lies in the angler's ability to read the water signs. Fish like bream, perch and pike, for instance, like to live in the quieter reaches away from the main flow of the current. Consequently if you want to try to catch any of these fish you should seek out the slack water behind islands or the slow eddies that are often found close to the bank. Roach, dace and chub on the other hand prefer to feed farther out in the stream but even these active fish seldom venture into the full force of the current and the only coarse fish which thrives in really fast water is the powerfully built barbel. During the autumn and winter months when the river is in flood, things change a little and then most species can be found in the deep sheltered holes right under the bank.

Many anglers believe that only large rivers are capable of producing big fish. Consequently, many side streams and small overgrown waterways are completely neglected. This is a pity, for many very big fish live in these small well-covered rivers.

Small waters are not easy to fish and before you can be successful you must learn to fish with the utmost caution. For this kind of angling a worm fished on floatless, leadless tackle makes a very good bait. In these overgrown waters it is a good idea to start at the lower end of the stretch and work steadily upstream, casting the bait upstream as you go. Bites are usually very determined affairs and more often than not the fish hook themselves with their first savage pull. If any extra weight is needed a small split shot or a twist of lead wire can be added to the line (Bottom right).

DACE

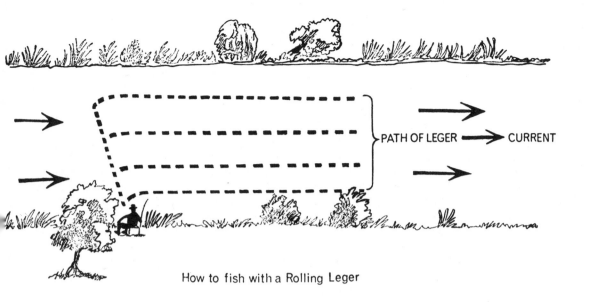

How to fish with a Rolling Leger

Places to find fish in rivers

UPSTREAM WORM

Spinning—1

Spinning is probably the most sporting method of catching pike and perch and in the hands of an expert it can be a beautiful and deadly art. Like all branches of angling it requires considerable practice to become a good spin fisherman. The three most essential things to learn about spinning are: (A) complete and absolute control of the tackle; (B) a sound knowledge of the fish and the water; and (C) a lack of fear of losing artificial baits. This last is probably the hardest, for it is difficult to deliberately cast an expensive lure into a snagged up piece of water. To catch decent fish consistently you must be prepared to risk losing a few baits.

Artificial lures are legion and there are now so many patterns available that it is extremely difficult to choose a suitable selection. Also it is very easy to buy baits just because they look nice in the shop. This is pointless but many anglers cannot resist buying lures, and most of them have vast collections of baits which in all probability they will never even use.

Basically you can divide artificial lures into three sections, the first being comprised of baits which are designed to look as much like a fish as possible. Of these the old fashioned wagtail is still the best and these ungainly looking lures will often catch fish when all the more modern baits have failed.

The Devon Minnow is another good fish catcher, especially for big perch in reservoirs and gravel pits. Being heavy, Devons are easy to cast, and will still revolve even when being retrieved at slow speeds. This is important, for perch are often attracted to a bait which flutters along close to the bottom. A lighter version of the Devon Minnow is the quill or Phantom Minnow. This is a semi-translucent bait constructed either from a bird quill or a length of plastic tubing.

Spoon baits are normally made from metal and in many parts of the country they are extremely popular among pike fishermen. They are obtainable in a wide variety of shapes, sizes and colours. For pike fishing a spoon with a length of around $3\frac{1}{2}$ in. is a good size. This size is unsuitable for perch fishing and if you want to concentrate entirely on perch choose a lure with a length of between $1\frac{1}{2}$ and 2 in. Many spoon baits are brightly coloured and although this makes them look more attractive they are no better, if as good, as gold or silver coloured spoons. These are generally cheaper than the brightly painted baits and they will catch more fish as well. The silver baits are best used when the water is clear, while the gold ones catch best when the water is muddy or cloudy.

Plug baits originated in the U.S.A. but in recent years they have become very popular in this country and there is no doubt that under the right conditions they are wonderful fish catchers.

Unfortunately they are rather expensive, particularly if you purchase the beautifully finished plastic plugs. Wooden ones are also available and these normally cost less than half the price of the plastic ones. Plugs can be obtained either as floaters or slow sinkers. The floating patterns are excellent for use in the weedy snag-ridden shallows, while the slow sinking type can be used in deeper water. The principle of the plug bait is that a vane or lip on the bait provides the action. The faster the bait is retrieved the more it will wriggle and dive.

PERCH

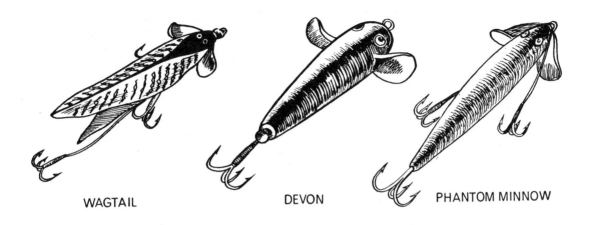

WAGTAIL   DEVON   PHANTOM MINNOW

SPOONS

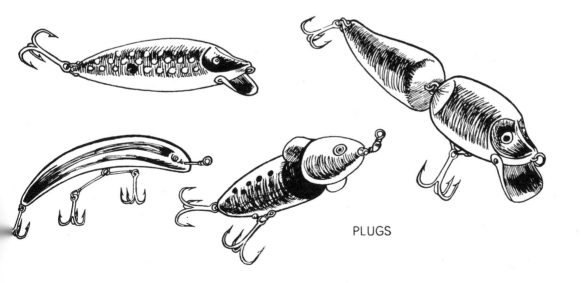

PLUGS

Spinning—2

Although all artificial lures are designed either to spin, wobble or dive through the water, it is still necessary to give them a more life-like movement. This can best be achieved by an irregular speed-of-retrieve, coupled with a side to side or up and down motion of the rod tip. Probably the best of all movements is the one known as the sink and draw technique. Here the bait is cast out and allowed to sink to the bottom, then when it has settled the rod tip should be lifted and the reel handle rapidly turned two or three times. This will cause the bait to dart upwards 2 or 3 ft. and then when you stop reeling it will flutter down again until it reaches the bottom. This makes it look very much like a small injured fish and most predators find a bait worked in this fashion almost irresistible.

Very often a pike or big perch will follow a bait right in almost to your feet. If you happen to notice a fish following the lure in this fashion do not slow down the rate of retrieve, instead increase it slightly, so that the bait suddenly darts forward. This will make it look just like a small fish trying to make a desperate dash for safety. Pike are particularly susceptible to these tactics and will usually put on a rapid spurt to catch up with and take the bait.

A slight variation on this technique is the "Fluttering Spoon". This works on a similar principle to the sink and draw method, except that the bait is retrieved steadily to start with and then every once in a while it is allowed to flutter down until it just touches bottom. As soon as you feel it touch down, however, you should immediately start to reel in again until you feel that the time is ripe to allow the spoon to sink downwards once more. Perch often show great interest in these tactics.

Very occasionally, while spinning for perch, you will feel the fish playfully "pluck" at the bait, without making any really determined effort to take it. This can be very frustrating and I have only found one way of overcoming this problem. This is a method which can be called the "Static spoon technique" for basically it is a variation of the Fluttering Spoon method, the difference being that when the bait touches the bottom it should be left there for anything up to 60 seconds before starting to retrieve it again.

A natural minnow fished Sink and Draw style is a very good bait and will catch perch and pike under a wide variety of conditions. The terminal tackle required for this method consists of a 9-in. trace, made from either nylon or fine wire, a size 8 or 10 treble hook, a swivel and a small drilled bullet. The illustration on the opposite page shows just how you should bait up with the minnow.

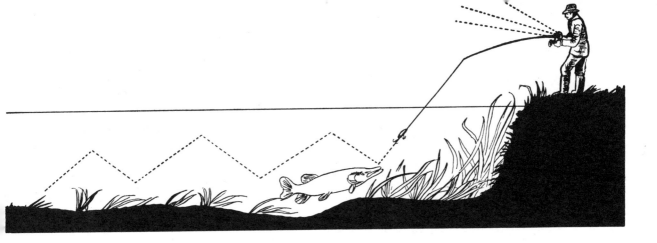

Giving the lure life

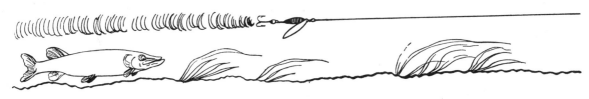

Steady retrieve

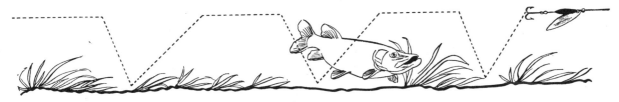

Sink and Draw

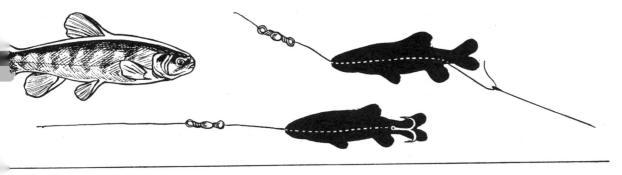

Sink and draw with a natural Minnow

Spinning—3

A standard method of spinning for pike is done with a natural bait mounted either on an Archer Spinner or on Wobble tackle. Usually a bait mounted on an Archer Spinner is on the small side, favourites being 6 in. roach, dace or bleak. Archer Spinners are obtainable from all tackle shops and with half a dozen of these and a dozen or so small dead baits you are all set up for a day's pike spinning. A bait mounted on an "Archer" flight spins in a conventional manner while a bait fished on "Wobble" tackle will sweep round in wide attractive spirals. The amount of wobble can easily be regulated by the degree of curve at the bait's tail. It is difficult to ascertain just what degree of "wobble" is required on each different water but a few experiments will quickly show just how much is needed. Most of the Norfolk anglers who employ this method use a very large bait, and rather than waste time trying to catch enough 9 or 10 in. roach or rudd for bait, they usually buy a pound or two of fresh herrings from their local wet fish shop. Always make sure, however, that the fish are fresh, for pike don't like a stinking bait. Also, when a fish starts to decompose, it naturally becomes soft, and in this state it will quickly break up during casting.

It always pays to spin a spot thoroughly. If you just make three or four casts and dash off to a new position you may miss fish. Once you have taken up your stance, search the water in front of you thoroughly, firstly with short casts to the right and then fanwise across your front and to the left. When you have searched this water, increase your length and do the same thing again.

Pike rely upon ambushing much of their food and as a rule they like to lurk among reed beds or lily pads, in the hope that some unsuspecting fish will come within reach of their huge tooth-filled jaws. Consequently it pays to work an artificial bait close to any likely weed beds. Normally this means that you will have to fish from a boat and if this is the case you must take great care not to frighten the fish by taking the boat too close to the weeds.

Keith Linsell

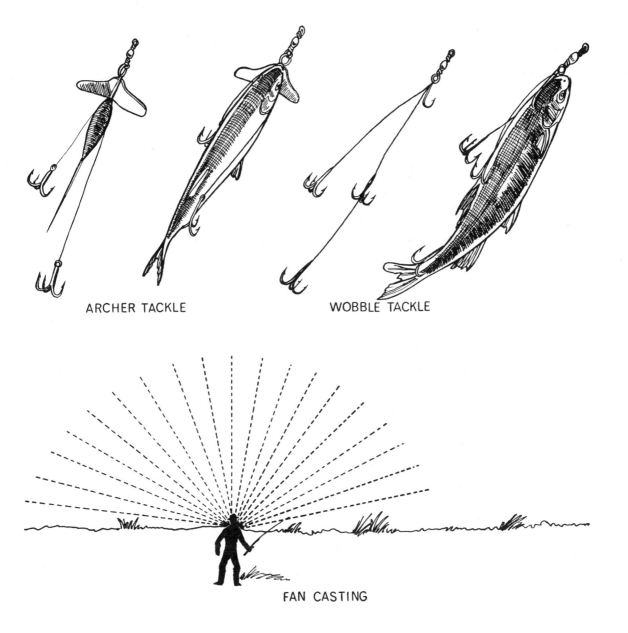

ARCHER TACKLE

WOBBLE TACKLE

FAN CASTING

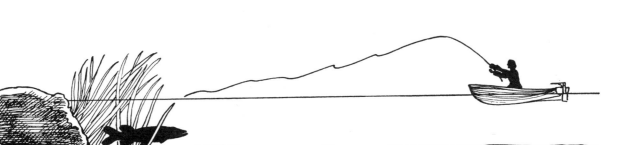

BOAT FISHING

Fly Fishing

Fly fishing for coarse fish can be a fascinating and rewarding occupation and even on hard fished waters you can usually be sure of some good sport, particularly if you fish during the late evenings, for at this time of the day many fish feed actively on the surface. The best fly rods are made of split cane. These are expensive. Hollow glass fly rods, on the other hand, are very cheap in comparison and three or four pounds will purchase a beautiful 9 ft. two-piece rod. There is no point in paying for an expensive fly reel because a cheap centre-pin will do the job perfectly well at a fraction of the cost. A fly line, however, is an expensive item and it pays to buy a good one. Cheap lines are available but they wear out quickly. For general fly fishing a plain straightforward level silk line is quite adequate. Silk lines should always be dried after use or they will become sticky and useless. Flies can be "wet" or "dry". The term "wet" denotes that the lure should be worked under the surface; dry flies are designed to float, and where possible these are tied to resemble natural insects. Although there are thousands of trout flies on the market half a dozen patterns are enough for coarse fish. Recommended patterns are: Coachman, Alder, Greenwell's Glory, Olive Dun, Coch-y-Bondhu and Olive Quill. These can be obtained either as wet or dry flies and half a dozen of each will last throughout the season.

How to cast a fly

The simplest way of explaining a standard fly casting technique is by diagrams. The six drawings on the opposite page explain the six movements needed to throw a fly. In position (A) the rod tip is dropped down towards the line, then using the forearm and the wrist the rod tip should be moved rapidly up to position (B), then without a pause the movement should be carried through to the (C) position. A brief pause is now called for. This allows the rod to straighten up which automatically pulls the line up behind the caster. The weight of the line then pulls the rod tip back into the (D) position. Next the rod is brought back through position (E) until it finishes up in the (F) position. It is essential not to start this forward movement until the line has straightened out behind you. To make sure that this happens you should look back over your shoulder and watch the line as it flies out behind you. If the forward motion is started before the line is fully extended the resulting jerk will break or "crack" off the fly.

The most important part of fly casting is the timing, and it must be remembered that the longer the line you have out the longer the pause before the rod is brought back down to the (F) position.

If more line is required to reach a rising fish you must "shoot" the line. This is not difficult and is done by pulling line from the reel with the left hand until the required amount has been stripped away. Then once the forward movement is almost completed this extra line should be released so that it shoots out through the rings and so lengthens the cast. For coarse fishing a single fly is sufficient, attached to a length of 5 lb. b.s. nylon cast. When a fish rises to the fly always give it a second to suck the bait in, and turn down with it. If you strike at the first splash you will usually miss your fish.

Keith Linsell

FLY ROD

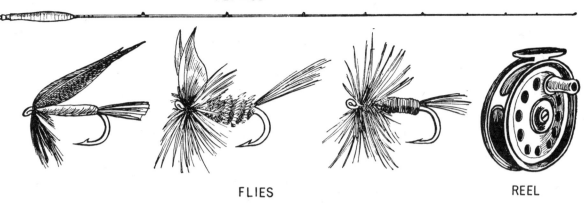

FLIES   REEL

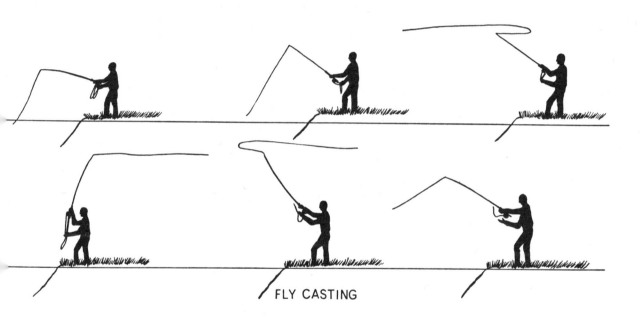

FLY CASTING

When to strike at a rising fish